TEACHING MATHEMATICS CREATIVELY

Are you looking for new ideas to capture the reluctant maths pupils in your class?

How can story, drama and GIANTS help you teach maths?

Teaching Mathematics Creatively is crammed full of practical approaches for bringing the teaching of mathematics to life. From an examination of where maths is failing to engage pupils in the twenty-first century, to a wide range of exciting approaches and ideas for ensuring it is possible to teach in a creative way, this is a stimulating and enjoyable source of inspiration for busy teachers.

It promotes creativity as a key element to develop young children's knowledge, understanding and enjoyment of mathematics and offers a range of strategies to enable teachers to take a playful approach to mathematics teaching. Imaginative ideas include.

- The power of story-telling and play to bring the subject alive for children and teachers alike
- Learning maths outdoors – work on a larger scale, make more noise, make more mess!
- Making sense of the numbers, patterns, shapes and measures children see around them every day
- Motivating children through problem finding and problem solving
- Using music, rhythm and pattern to teach maths creatively
- Giant maths – how much food does a giant need in a week?

Underpinned by the latest research and theory and with contemporary and cutting edge practice at the forefront, *Teaching Mathematics Creatively* includes a wealth of innovative ideas to enthuse teachers and enrich mathematics teaching. It is an essential purchase for every teacher who wishes to employ creative approaches to teaching in their classroom.

Lind[illegible]d has great educational experience and has published extensively in the fields [illegible]ning and creative maths. She is an Early Years Education Consultant and a reg[illegible] contributor to *Nursery World*.

Trisha Lee is Founder and Artistic Director of MakeBelieve Arts, a social enterprise offering innovative, high quality theatre and education programmes to develop the creative potential [illegible] children aged 2 to 15, based in [illegible] London, UK.

LEARNING TO TEACH IN THE PRIMARY SCHOOL SERIES

Series Editor: Teresa Cremin, the Open University

Teaching is an art form. It demands not only knowledge and understanding of the core areas of learning, but also the ability to teach these creatively and effectively and foster learner creativity in the process. *The Learning to Teach in the Primary School Series* draws upon recent research, which indicates the rich potential of creative teaching and learning, and explores what it means to teach creatively in the primary phase. It also responds to the evolving nature of the subject teaching in a wider, more imaginatively framed twenty-first century primary curriculum.

Designed to complement the textbook *Learning to Teach in the Primary School*, the well-informed, lively texts offer support for students and practising teachers who want to develop more flexible and responsive creative approaches to teaching and learning. The books highlight the importance of teachers' own creative engagement and share a wealth of innovative ideas to enrich pedagogy and practice.

Titles in the series:

Teaching English Creatively
Teresa Cremin

Teaching Maths Creatively
Linda Pound and Trisha Lee

Teaching Science Creatively
Dan Davies

TEACHING MATHEMATICS CREATIVELY

Linda Pound

and

Trisha Lee

Routledge
Taylor & Francis Group
LONDON AND NEW YORK

This first edition published 2011
by Routledge
2 Park Square, Milton Park, Abingdon, Oxon, OX14 4RN

Simultaneously published in the USA and Canada
by Routledge
711 Third Avenue, New York, NY 10017

Routledge is an imprint of the Taylor & Francis Group, an informa business

Typeset in Times New Roman and Helvetica Neue by
Florence Production Ltd, Stoodleigh, Devon
Printed and bound in Great Britain by
TJ International Ltd, Padstow, Cornwall

British Library Cataloguing in Publication Data
A catalogue record for this book is available from the British Library

Library of Congress Cataloging-in-Publication Data
Pound, Linda.
Teaching mathematics creatively/by Linda Pound and Trisha Lee.
– 1st ed.
p. cm.
1. Mathematics – Study and teaching (Secondary). 2. Curriculum planning.
3. Lesson planning. I. Lee, Trisha. II. Title.
QA11.P6325 2011
510.71 – dc22 2010017480

ISBN13: 978–0–415–57591–1 (hbk)
ISBN13: 978–0–415–57592–8 (pbk)
ISBN13: 978–0–203–84050–4 (ebk)

CONTENTS

TABLES

ACKNOWLEDGEMENTS

The authors would like to thank the staff and creative associates at MakeBelieve Arts for allowing us to incorporate several case studies that are drawn directly from the company's work. We would particularly like to thank Jen Lunn and Isla Tompsett for their creative input into the development of the Creative Approaches to Mathematics programme at MakeBelieve Arts. Thanks are also due to Jeannie Hughes and her staff for their contribution and their positive and creative approach!

PREFACE

Over the last two decades, teachers in England, working in a culture of accountability and target setting, have been required to introduce both the National Curriculum and the literacy and numeracy strategies; both content and pedagogy have been specified. Positioned as passive recipients of the prescribed agenda, it could be argued that practitioners have had their hands tied, their voices quietened and their professional autonomy threatened and constrained. In order to conform to expectations and deliver the imposed curriculum, research reveals that some teachers short-changed their principles and their knowledge and understanding of pedagogy and practice (English *et al*. 2002; Burns and Myhill 2004). The relentless quest for higher standards and curriculum coverage which dominated this period may well have obscured the personal and affective dimensions of teaching and learning and fostered a mindset characterised more by compliance and conformity than curiosity and creativity.

Recently however, creativity and creative policies and practices have become prominent in government policy alongside the standards agenda and a focus on creative teaching and learning has been in evidence. Heralded by the publication *All Our Futures: Creativity, Culture and Education* (NACCCE 1999), this shift is exemplified in the Creative Partnerships initiative, in the Qualifications and Curriculum Authority's creativity framework (QCA 2005) and in a plethora of reports (e.g. Ofsted 2003; DfES 2003; CAPEUK 2006;Ofsted 2006; Roberts 2006; DCMS 2006). The definition of creativity employed by most of these documents is that coined in *All Our Futures,* namely that creativity is 'imaginative activity fashioned so as to produce outcomes that are both original and of value' (NACCCE 1999: 30). As a new decade commences, schools continue to be exhorted to be more innovative in curriculum construction and the coalition government plans to introduce primary phase academies, which will apparently be formally afforded increased freedom and the opportunity to shape their own curricula. Yet for primary educators, tensions persist, not only because the dual policies of performativity and creativity appear contradictory, but also because in recent years they have been positioned more as technically competent curriculum deliverers, rather than artistically engaged, research-informed curriculum developers. I believe, alongside Eisner (2003) and others, that teaching is an art form and that teachers benefit from viewing themselves as versatile artists in the classroom, drawing on their personal passions and creativity as they research their practice. As Joubert observes:

> Creative teaching is an art. One cannot teach teachers didactically how to be creative; there is no fail safe recipe or routines. Some strategies may help to promote creative thinking, but teachers need to develop a full repertoire of skills which they can adapt to different situations.
>
> (Joubert 2001: 21)

However, creative teaching is only part of the picture, since teaching for creativity also needs to be acknowledged and their mutual dependency recognised. The former focuses more on teachers using imaginative approaches in the classroom in order to make learning more interesting and effective, the latter, more on the development of children's creativity (NACCCE 1999). Both rely upon an understanding of the notion of creativity and demand that professionals confront the myths and mantras which surround the word. These include the commonly held misconceptions that creativity is connected only to participation in the arts and that it is confined to particular individuals, a competence of a few specially gifted children.

Creativity is an allusive concept, which has been multiply defined by educationalists, psychologists and neurologists, as well as by policy makers in different countries and cultural contexts. Debates resound about its individual and/or collaborative nature, the degree to which it is generic or domain specific, and the difference between the 'Big C' creativity of genius and the 'little c' creativity of the everyday. Notwithstanding these issues, most scholars in the field perceive it involves the capacity to generate, reason and critically evaluate novel ideas and/or imaginary scenarios. As such, I perceive it encompasses thinking through and solving problems, making connections, inventing and reinventing and flexing one's imaginative muscles in all aspects of learning and life.

In the primary classroom, creative teaching and learning have been associated with innovation, originality, ownership and control (Woods and Jeffrey 1996; Jeffrey 2006) and creative teachers have been seen, in their planning and teaching and in the ethos which they create, to afford high value to curiosity and risk taking, to ownership, autonomy and making connections (Cremin 2009; Cremin *et al*. 2009). Such teachers, it has been posited, often work in partnership with others: with children, other teachers and experts from beyond the school gates (Cochrane and Cockett 2007). Additionally, in research exploring possibility thinking, which it is argued is at the heart of creativity in education (Craft 2000), an intriguing interplay between teachers and children has been observed; both were involved in possibility thinking their ways forwards and in immersing themselves in playful contexts, posing questions, being imaginative, showing self-determination, taking risks and innovating (Burnard *et al*. 2006; Cremin *et al*. 2006). A new pedagogy of possibility beckons.

This series *Learning to Teach in the Primary School*, which accompanies and complements the edited textbook *Learning to Teach in the Primary School* (Arthur and Cremin 2010), seeks to support teachers in developing as creative practitioners, assisting them in exploring the synergies and potential of teaching creatively and teaching for creativity. The series does not merely offer practical strategies for use in the classroom, though these abound, but more importantly seeks to widen teachers' and student teachers' knowledge and understanding of the principles underpinning a creative approach to teaching, principles based on research. It seeks to mediate the wealth of research evidence and make accessible and engaging the diverse theoretical perspectives and scholarly arguments available, demonstrating their practical relevance and value to the profession. Those who aspire to develop further as creative and curious educators will, I trust, find much of value in the series to support their own professional learning journeys and markedly enrich their pedagogy and practice right across the curriculum.

TERESA CREMIN

Teresa Cremin (Grainger) is a Professor of Education (Literacy) at the Open University and a past President of UKRA (2001–2) and UKLA (2007–9). She is currently co-convenor of the BERA Creativity SIG and a trustee of Booktrust, The Poetry Archive and UKLA. Her work involves research, publication and consultancy in literacy and creativity. Her current projects seek to explore children's everyday lives and literacy practices, teachers' identities as readers and writers and the characteristics and associated pedagogy that fosters possibility thinking within creative learning in the primary years. Teresa has published widely, writing and co-editing a variety of books including: *Teaching English Creatively* (Routledge 2009); *Learning to Teach in the Primary School* (Routledge 2010); *Jumpstart Drama* (David Fulton 2009); *Documenting Creative Learning 5–11* (Trentham 2007); *Creativity and Writing: Developing Voice and Verve* (Routledge 2005); *Teaching English in Higher Education* (NATE and UKLA 2007); *Creative Activities for Character, Setting and Plot, 5–7, 7–9, 9–11* (Scholastic 2004); and *Language and Literacy: A Routledge Reader* (Routledge 2001).

REFERENCES

Arthur, J. and Cremin, T. (2010) (eds.) *Learning to Teach in the Primary School* (2nd edition), London: Routledge.

Burnard, P., Craft, A. and Cremin, T. (2006) 'Possibility thinking', *International Journal of Early Years Education,* 14(3): 243–62.

Burns, C. and Myhill, D. (2004) 'Interactive or inactive? A consideration of the nature of interaction in whole class teaching', *Cambridge Journal of Education*, 34: 35–49.

CapeUK (2006) *Building Creative Futures: The Story of Creative Action Research Awards, 2004–2005*. London: Arts Council.

Cohrane, P. and Cockett, M. (2007) *Building a Creative School: A Dynamic Approach to School Development*. London: Trentham.

Craft, A. (2000). *Creativity Across the Primary Curriculum*. London: Routledge.

Cremin, T. (2009) 'Creative teaching and creative teachers', in A. Wilson (ed.) *Creativity in Primary Education*. Exeter: Learning Matters, pp. 36–46.

Cremin, T., Burnard, P. and Craft, A. (2006). 'Pedagogy and possibility thinking in the early years', *International Journal of Thinking Skills and Creativity*, 1(2): 108–19.

Cremin, T., Barnes, J. and Scoffham, S. (2009) *Creative Teaching for Tomorrow: Fostering a Creative State of Mind*. Deal: Future Creative.

Department for Education and Skills (DfES) (2003) *Excellence and Enjoyment: A Strategy for Primary Schools*. Nottingham: DfES.

Department for Culture, Media and Sport (2006). *Government Response to Paul Roberts' Report on Nurturing Creativity in Young People*. London: DCMS.

Eisner, E. (2003) 'Artistry in education', *Scandinavian Journal of Educational Research*, 47(3): 373–84.

English, E., Hargreaves, L. and Hislam, J. (2002) 'Pedagogical dilemmas in the National Literacy Strategy: primary teachers' perceptions, reflections and classroom behaviour', *Cambridge Journal of Education*, 32(1): 9–26.

Jeffrey, B. (ed.) (2006) *Creative Learning Practices: European Experiences*. London: Tufnell Press.

Joubert, M. M. (2001) 'The art of creative teaching: NACCCE and beyond', in A. Craft, B. Jeffrey and M. Liebling (eds) *Creativity in Education*. London: Continuum.

National Advisory Committee on Creative and Cultural Education (NACCCE) (1999) *All Our Futures: Creativity, Culture and Education*. London: Department for Education and Employment.

Ofsted (2003) *Expecting the Unexpected: Developing Creativity in Primary and Secondary Schools*, HMI 1612. E-publication. Available at http://www.ofsted.gov.uk (accessed 9th November 2007).

Ofsted (2006) 'Ofsted inspection of creative partnerships', available at http://www.creative-partnerships.com/aboutcp/businessevidence (Accessed 14th May 2007).

Qualifications and Curriculum Authority (QCA) (2005). *Creativity: Find It, Promote It! – Promoting Pupils' Creative Thinking and Behaviour Across The Curriculum At Key Stages 1, 2 And 3 – Practical Materials For Schools*. London: QCA.

Roberts, P. (2006) *Nurturing Creativity in Young People. A Report to Government to Inform Future Policy*. London: DCMS.

Woods, P. and Jeffrey, B. (1996) *Teachable Moments: The Art of Creative Teaching in Primary Schools*. Buckingham: Open University Press.

CHAPTER 1 INTRODUCTION: WHAT IS CREATIVE MATHEMATICS?

INTRODUCTION

Faced with the question 'what counts as mathematics?', many people will respond by talking about numbers and sums. In the past, most people were taught mathematics by rote and either failed or succeeded. Success as a mathematician offered high academic status but, perversely, any apparent failure as a mathematician has not carried the stigma that not being able to read or write carries. While illiterate adults adopt all manner of strategies to hide their inability, innumerate adults will happily declare that they can't do maths to save their lives!

A wide range of research has highlighted the fact that humans are born with a wide range of mathematical competences (Butterworth 1999, 2005; Dehaene 1997; Devlin 2000). This is strangely at odds with the fact that for many years, a significant proportion of the adult population has been functionally innumerate (see for example Boaler 2009). The Cockcroft Report, for example, published in 1982 (DES 1982), highlighted then current concerns about low standards of mathematical achievement, but also reported that such anxieties had existed for well over a century before that. The introduction of the National Curriculum (DfEE 1999a) was intended to raise standards and to ensure entitlement to a broad and balanced curriculum. The entitlement for mathematics included number (including, at Key Stage 2, algebra); and shape, space and measures. Handling data was added to this at Key Stage 2. The programme of study for mathematics (DfEE 1999a) emphasised the ways in which mathematics is linked to spiritual, moral, social and cultural development. It also underlined the integral key skills and cross-curricular nature of mathematics.

However, the introduction of the National Numeracy Strategy (NNS) (DfEE 1999b) and the nature of the Standard Assessment Tasks (SATs) shifted the focus back to a narrower perception of what mathematics is. In an international test of the mathematical understanding of everyday maths of 15-year-olds, UK students came 8th in 2000 but 24th in 2007 (Boaler 2009). This is particularly perplexing when the term numeracy as adopted by the NNS apparently seeks to emphasise those aspects of mathematics which are needed to manage everyday life. The NNS framework (DfEE

1999b: 4) defines numeracy as 'a proficiency which involves confidence and competence with numbers and measures'. The document further suggests that numeracy involves an ability to compute numbers, including an understanding of the number system; an ability and motivation to solve number problems and an understanding of the ways in which mathematical information can be collected and presented.

Predictably SATs came to focus on the elements of the curriculum that are more readily assessed. But these elements, while of vital importance, are by no means all that mathematics is. Boaler (2009) has called the mathematics that is taught in school 'fake mathematics'. She underlines the differences between 'real mathematics' (both as it is understood by ordinary people and by mathematicians) and the mathematics that is taught in school. She stresses that there is an urgent need to address the gap.

SO WHAT IS MATHEMATICS?

Mathematics has been described as 'the abstract key which turns the lock of the physical universe' (Devlin 2002: 10, citing Polkinhorne). Devlin (2000, 2002) simply describes mathematics as the *science of patterns*. Guy Claxton, in his submission to the Cambridge Primary Review (Alexander 2010: 224), argues that the high status given to mathematics is based on a false premise derived from the legacy of the classical emphasis on logical and 'quasi-logical' thinking which has long dominated Western education. This presents mathematics, erroneously in Claxton's view, as a subject which:

- is timeless and does not therefore need to be relevant
- may be broken down into segments which can be taught in isolation through graded exercises
- can be organised in such a way as to ensure that there are clear right and wrong answers, making it simple to assess.

For Claxton this approach to mathematics is 'a million miles away' from 'the real way mathematicians actually solve problems and make discoveries' (Alexander 2010: 224, citing Claxton). Similarly, Worthington and Carruthers (2006: 222) compare young children's attempts to learn mathematics to those of someone learning a new language. They suggest that children need to become much more than mere 'adders and dividers'. What society actually needs, they argue, are 'seekers and solvers of problems and makers of new mathematical meanings'.

Mathematics is a vital part of human endeavour at many levels. At an unconscious level it is what enables:

- a baby to match two sounds to two objects, or to recognise errors when a small number of toys are added or removed from another group of toys (Pound 2006)
- a golfer to judge the distance he or she must hit the ball
- snooker players to get the white ball ricocheting off the coloured balls at exactly the correct angle

- a cook to estimate the timings to ensure that all elements of a meal are ready at the same time
- all of us to cross the road safely.

The subject includes some mundane and perhaps downright boring elements. Knowing number bonds and tables by heart is often seen as an essential part – yet not all mathematicians are good at remembering these facts. Marcus du Sautoy, the Simonyl Professor for the Public Understanding of Science and a professor of mathematics at Oxford University, declares, for example:

> Times tables. You know, I'm not terribly fast at my times tables, because that's not what I think mathematics is about. I think it's the same thing as thinking that a good speller will make a great writer. Well, no, actually – great writers can be crap at spelling, but have great vision and ways of bringing stories alive – and I think you've got to put over that mathematics is a similar idea.
>
> (du Sautoy 2008a)

Conversely some highly skilled and intuitive users of mathematics do not regard themselves as mathematicians at all. Nunes *et al.* (1993) offer examples of street sellers in South America – young boys able to execute complex sums in their heads as they sell fruit and give change. Parallel everyday experiences for many of us may include darts players able to work out which number they must next hit, or gamblers working out complicated odds on horses or dogs winning a race. Yet offered pencil and paper to support their calculations, many of these skilled users of mathematical strategies and ideas would have great difficulty in coming up with a sensible answer to the very same problems.

We are told that in an increasingly technological world, an understanding of mathematics becomes ever more important (du Sautoy 2010; Boaler 2009; Devlin 2002). Understanding of our world demands what is often called 'mathematical literacy'. The Organisation for Economic Co-operation and Development (OECD) uses the term mathematical literacy defining it as:

> the capacity to identify, to understand and to engage in mathematics and make well-founded judgements about the role that mathematics plays, as needed for an individual's current and future private life, occupational life, social life with peers and relatives, and life as a constructive, concerned, and reflective citizen.
>
> (OECD 1999: 50)

This view of mathematics is perhaps richer than that offered by NNS and involves being able to understand something of how statistical statements and mathematical claims are arrived at and what they actually mean. This is certainly a far cry from the mathematics that was demanded in Victorian times when compulsory schooling was introduced. It is not enough to be able to add up columns of figures – we have machines to do that – but it is vital that children are able to calculate quickly and with some degree of accuracy in everyday situations – with confidence.

Perhaps more important than being able to compute – add, subtract, multiply or divide – is an ability to estimate an answer, using common sense (Pound 2006; Devlin 2000). Boaler (2009: 26) comments on the difficulties which face many children when asked to estimate: 'they have not developed a good *feel* for numbers which would enable them to estimate instead of calculate . . . they have learned, wrongly, that mathematics is all about precision, not about making estimates or guesses.'

Then there are writers who emphasise the world of mathematics which is fascinating and beautiful, puzzling and exciting. This world is often described by those who experienced it as children. Seymour Papert's subsequent passion for mathematics which led him to develop Logo, an early piece of software which enabled young children to program the movements of a 'turtle', began with a consuming interest in cogs. After visiting a mill in early childhood he, by his own admission, became obsessed with the idea of ratio (Papert 1982). Shakuntala Devi, described in the *Guinness Book of Records* as a 'human computer', considers mathematics to be a thing of beauty and entertainment. She writes:

> At three I fell in love with numbers. It was sheer ecstasy for me to do sums and get the right answers. Numbers were toys with which I could play . . . My interest grew with age. I took immense delight in working out huge problems mentally – sometimes even faster than electronic calculating machines and computers . . . All along I had cherished a desire to show those who think mathematics boring and dull just how beautiful it can be.
>
> (Devi 1977: 9)

This enthusiasm is also described by mathematicians keen to share their interest. Carol Vorderman (2010) describes her excitement about numbers as coming from the way in which they dance in her head. Marcus du Sautoy describes the many and varied functional uses of mathematics and concludes that his interest in mathematics was motivated by:

> the sheer beauty of the ideas, structures and new ways of looking at the world. A world without knowing about primes, symmetry and 4D geometry would be like never hearing Mozart, seeing Picasso, or experiencing Shakespeare. A world without maths would be impoverished politically, technologically, scientifically and culturally.
>
> (du Sautoy 2010: 7)

Keith Devlin, journalist and professor of mathematics, shares this broader view. He states that:

> mathematics is not about number, but about life. It is about the world in which we live. It is about ideas. And, far from being dull and sterile as it is so often portrayed it is full of creativity.
>
> (Devlin 2000: 76)

Of course, mathematics is about number – but it is about other things too. In 2009, the National Strategy produced an article entitled 'So what is mathematics?' (National Strategy 2009). Five aspects are highlighted:

- Mathematics builds from simple definitions and propositions that are based on observation.
- Mathematics involves measuring, comparing and classifying objects.
- Mathematics describes patterns, properties and general concepts.
- Mathematics provides the tools to abstract and work in an imagined world.
- Mathematics is a creative subject in which ideas can be generated, tested and refined.

There are some interesting ideas within these statements. The idea of mathematics being based on observation is not one which has been widely acknowledged within mathematics education – and yet of course this is where mathematics came from. Humans noticed relationships between various objects (Cairns 2007; Brandt 2009) and used these as symbols. Fingers and footsteps, moons and stars all served to support the development of early human mathematical understanding.

The algorithms for addition and subtraction, multiplication and division evolved in order to help us measure and compare, yet somehow this has been lost as confused children faced with a mathematical problem enquire 'is it an add or a take away?' The notion of mathematics as a tool for classifying is also often lost. In the early years, for example, practitioners become anxious about children who 'don't know their colours' and see this as a failure in mathematical understanding. Of course it's useful to be able to tell red from yellow, but it is not an inherently mathematical idea. Let's be equally interested in children who know their colours and those who can differentiate engine sounds – able to tell you whether they are hearing a Ford or Volkswagen.

In education, pattern has been a much neglected element of mathematics. It is found in numbers and counting, in shape, in motion, reasoning, probability and topology (Devlin 2002). Devlin (2000) describes the patterns and relationships studied by mathematicians as occurring in nature, knots, planets, animal fur and birds' feathers, in voting, games, the structure of language and in music. The patterns frequently involve things that are not yet visible – either in helping to predict events or in considering ideas such as the Big Bang. Devlin (2002) argues that as we seek and find patterns we begin to make the 'invisible visible'.

Imagination is not a word which is readily associated with mathematics by the average man or woman in the street. It is, however, increasingly understood to be a vital element of mathematical thinking. Mathematics involves a great deal of abstract thought – from the earliest days, just thinking about 'two' is an abstraction. Devlin (2000) suggests that mathematics is the most abstract subject – but that may be because he is a mathematician! Whether or not mathematics is more abstract than other disciplines, thinking in the abstract involves imagination. A range of research suggests that abstract mathematical thinking has at its roots imagination. Devlin writes:

> The key to being able to think mathematically is to push this ability to 'fake reality' one step further into a realm that is purely symbolic . . . Mathematicians learn how to live in and reason about a purely symbolic world . . . created in the mind.
>
> (Devlin 2000: 120)

Equally alien to popular thinking about mathematics is the idea that it is a creative subject. Many writers have made this link. Mazur (2003: 225) cites Kant in saying that 'mathematics is pure poetry'. Thoreau echoes and extends that idea when he writes, perhaps a little cynically, that 'we have heard much about the poetry of mathematics, but very little of it has yet been sung' (cited by Pound 2006: 42). This is an idea which will be explored throughout this book. We hope by the end of it that you will not only recognise mathematics as a creative subject but be ready to help more of it to be sung – by teaching this creative subject creatively!

WHAT DO WE MEAN BY CREATIVITY?

Whole books have been written trying to define creativity. Ramachandran and Blakeslee (1999: 197) have described it as the 'ineffable quality' that makes us human. It is, however, a term which is widely used in education, but not always with the same sense of existential qualities. Alexander (2010) states that the words 'creative' and 'creativity' appeared more frequently in submissions to the Cambridge Primary Review than any others. Anna Craft, in her submission to the committee, reminds us that:

> The very nature of creativity in education remains ambiguous. To what extent creativity in primary education is conceived of as involving creative partnerships, as opposed simply to valuing and nourishing children's ideas in multiple contexts, is not clear. To what extent collective or collaborative creativity is valued as against individualized models, is also unclear; similarly there are still slippages in language between 'creative teaching', 'teaching for creativity' and 'creative learning'.
>
> (Craft, cited in Alexander 2010: 227)

Gardner (2006) suggests that creativity is a skill or attribute which will be much needed by society in the near future, but he reminds us that creativity has not always been welcomed. The early purposes of universal schooling were not to promote creativity but to prepare children for a life of routine. He writes that:

> In the past, creative individuals in a society were at best a mixed blessing – disdained, discouraged, even destroyed at the time of their breakthrough, possibly to be honored by posterity at some later point. Our time, our era is different.
>
> (Gardner 2006: 78)

Gardner (2006) criticizes the view of creativity, widely adopted in business, as being little more than lateral thinking (see for example de Bono 1995). He emphasises the importance of recognising the very varied nature of creativity, not simply *Big C* or *little c* creativity. Moreover a person creative in one area of endeavour is not necessarily creative in another. Gardner underlines the seminal view of Csikszentmihalyi (1997) that creativity emerges from an interaction of:

- an individual's mastery of a discipline and his or her willingness to modify or change current thinking in the area
- the cultural domain – ideas and models open to the creator
- the social field through which the creator's work or ideas are disseminated to a broader audience.

The test of creativity is summed up by Gardner, citing such notables as Einstein and Picasso, with the question 'has the domain in which you operate been significantly altered by your contribution?'

Clearly, strict adherence to this view of creativity would mean that creativity never occurred in the primary years of schooling and that would be far from the truth. Ken Robinson chaired the committee which produced a report on creativity in education for the government (NACCCE 1999). In that report, creativity was identified as having four key elements, namely imagination; reflection; originality; and a sense of purpose. In a subsequent publication, Robinson (2001) describes three levels of originality – personal, social and historic. Children are unlikely to produce work of historic originality but they will often produce things that are original for them and it is this that should be nurtured in school. Promoting collaboration is also likely to ensure the development of social originality – producing things new to a culture or group.

Gardner (2006: 84) suggests that prior to entering statutory schooling children are at the height of their creative powers. He suggests that the challenge for educators is 'to keep alive the mind and sensibility of the young child'. For Gardner, there is a simple recipe:

> for the nurturing of creating minds in the first decades of life. Following a period of open, untrammeled exploration in early childhood, it is indeed appropriate to master literacies and the disciplines . . . [E]ven during periods of drill, it is vital to keep open alternative possibilities and to foreground the option of unfettered exploration . . . [I]n the middle years of schooling, parents should make sure that their children pursue hobbies or activities which do not feature a single right answer . . . Teachers ought to illustrate the several ways in which a particular math problem can properly be solved . . . they ought to encourage youngsters to play games drawn from other cultures or to invent new games on the playground or on the computer.
>
> (Gardner 2006: 86–7)

MATHEMATICS AND CREATIVITY

It is apparent that mathematics is not generally well taught. It seems that the numeracy strategy and the primary national strategies have made some difference in raising standards in mathematics but not enough (Ofsted 2005; Boaler 2009). Robinson (2001: 4) suggests that change is needed in education because:

- *We are caught up in a social and economic revolution.* Robinson likens the change needed to the Industrial Revolution. When Charles Clarke introduced *Excellence and Enjoyment* (DfES 2003), he described it as ushering in a third revolution – the creative revolution, following the industrial and technological revolutions.
- *To survive it we need a new conception of human resources.* Current approaches to education and training are hampered by ideas of intelligence and creativity that have wasted untold talent and ability.
- *To develop these resources we need radically new strategies.* We won't survive the future simply by doing better what we have done in the past. Raising standards is no good if they're the wrong standards.

The aim of this book is to consider some approaches which might help to change the way in which mathematics is conceived, taught and learnt. Just as the term creativity has many meanings and interpretations, so the way in which the term can be applied to mathematics education also has many possibilities. Ways of *Teaching Mathematics Creatively* will be explored by focusing on a number of different aspects. These will include creative teaching; creative learning; creative partnerships and creative mathematics.

CREATIVE TEACHING

In order to teach creatively, teachers will use all their creative skills to plan and provide imaginative and stimulating activities, experiences and resources. Creative teaching will also involve promoting the creativity of children in order to develop their understanding. This may be through encouraging them to question or challenge what has been presented to them; to imagine other possibilities; and to make connections with other ideas or areas of learning; and to present their ideas in ways which promote critical reflection.

Ofsted (2010), in its review of creative partnerships, suggests that creative learning is supported by the following creative teaching strategies:

- cross-curricular learning and independent enquiry
- inclusive provision
- provision for experiential learning, involving first-hand, concrete experience
- technology integrated into teaching
- a planned enrichment programme – going beyond the National Curriculum entitlement
- links with the community and its cultures and a spirit of partnership
- flexible timetabling.

In *Excellence and Enjoyment* (DfES 2003: 27), it is reported that:

> teachers found that when they actively planned for and responded to pupils' creative ideas and actions, pupils became more curious to discover things for

themselves, were open to new ideas and keen to explore those ideas with the teacher and others. Promoting creativity is a powerful way of engaging pupils.

This view is echoed specifically in relation to teaching mathematics creatively by Upitis *et al.* (1997). They report a study in which cross-curricular and creative approaches to mathematics were tried out. Pimm (Upitis *et al.* 1997: xv), in his preface to the book, suggests to teachers that: 'This is not an enterprise that requires a complete upheaval in classroom setting . . . It is containable. But beware. The excitement of mathematical thinking is contagious: "hard fun" can prove addictive.'

This underlines the relationship between teaching and learning – important in many subjects but particularly so in mathematics where many adults and children alike have a poor attitude towards mathematics. This topic will be considered in more detail in the next chapter.

CREATIVE LEARNING

If it is difficult to define 'creativity', it is even more taxing to try to define 'creative learning'. It may be thought of as a way of thinking – like de Bono's lateral thinking. Alternatively it is sometimes thought of as a set of characteristics or attributes likely to be found in creative people. These may include risk-taking and flexibility or being more curious and more open to new ideas; demonstrating greater application and willingness to work with others (QCA 2005). Above all, of great importance in mathematics is the attribute of developing a 'what if?' learning disposition. As we will see in subsequent chapters, this disposition, sometimes termed 'conjectural thinking', is at the heart of problem-solving.

A further aspect of creative learning concerns the use of creative arts to symbolise, support and represent mathematical ideas. This is focal to the work of MakeBelieve Arts in developing creative approaches to mathematics. MakeBelieve Arts bases its philosophy on the following ideas – all of which will be explored in some detail throughout this book:

- Narrative supports learning (Paley 1990) even mathematical learning (Egan 1988) because it symbolises ideas and concepts and contextualises them.
- Symbolic representation in a range of different modes and media supports thinking and learning (Namy 2005; Malaguzzi 1995; Rogoff 2003; Egan 1991) across all intelligences, including mathematical intelligences (Gardner 1999).
- The imagination supports exploration of the boundaries between reality and unreality. Moreover it supports the development of abstract thought.
- Learning, including mathematical learning, requires that the learner goes beyond hard facts. It requires emotional engagement and motivation (Goleman 1996).

CREATIVE PARTNERSHIPS

Ofted's report on creative partnerships (2010) underlines the importance of what artists, including actors, designers, musicians and story-tellers, can bring to supporting children's achievement. The reported benefits that working with artists brings to children learning mathematics and science is, for many people, counter-intuitive. Why should focusing on creative arts help to improve children's understanding in other areas of the curriculum? We hope that this book will show the benefits and identify some of the reasons why this should be the case.

Gardner (2006: 86) offers some answers when he suggests that creativity can be fostered by:

> exhibiting different equally viable solutions to a single posed problem; exposing youngsters to attractive, creative persons who model both the approach and the experiences of the creative life; and introducing new pursuits that are removed from the academic treadmill and that reward innovation and look benignly on errors.

Gardner's comments are interesting when applied to mathematics. The primary national strategy and its predecessor the numeracy strategy have made strenuous efforts to ensure that the notion of a single right answer is challenged. Whether right or wrong, children are encouraged to explain their thinking – a strategy which can highlight the effectiveness of many different approaches. However, the notion of creative mathematicians coming into contact with children is an interesting one. In describing the work of a mathematician, Devlin (2000) emphasises an absence of deductive reasoning in the early stages of mathematical problem-solving. He highlights the experimentation, guessing, sweeping generalisations, intuition and 'unwarranted conclusions' which occur. He concludes with a description which is far from the popular understanding of what mathematics is and mathematicians do:

> Only after the mathematician thinks she has solved a problem does she start to work out a logical proof, a process that involves organizing the various ideas and insights that led to the solution into a precise, logical argument.
>
> (Devlin 2000: 253)

CREATIVE MATHEMATICS

Teaching mathematics creatively involves gaining an understanding of the creative nature of mathematics. Earlier in this chapter, reference was made to Marcus du Sautoy's claim that it is the beauty of mathematics which motivated him. Reference was also made to writers describing the poetry of mathematics. Mathematics is not a subject which is simply a set of right and wrong answers but one which requires conjecture – using imagination and guesswork, or even intuition (Claxton 1997). It requires a mindset which seeks out patterns and problems. It relies on abstract thought – linked as we have seen to imagination – but also relying on an ability to use 'symbols, images, diagrams and models as tools to support thinking' (National Strategies 2006: 6).

In considering the work of creative partnerships, Ofsted (2010) emphasises some of the characteristics of successful teaching leading to creativity. Table 1.1 identifies some of those characteristics with particular value for mathematics.

Table 1.1 Teaching strategies and creative mathematics

Characteristics of teaching successfully promoting creativity (National Strategies 2006)	Application to teaching mathematics
Teachers guided but did not over-direct pupils.	Mathematics education has a long history of being over-directive. We make assumptions that the rote elements must be in place before the creative element can be introduced. This has the effect of stultifying children's creative minds.
Considerable emphasis was placed on developing skills, especially problem-solving and communication, with pupils able to track their progress and to understand how one level of competence led on to the next.	Since problem-solving is key to mathematics this emphasis is vital.
Teachers' skills in questioning pupils were excellent. They fostered a spirit of enquiry and an awareness of there being multiple possibilities rather than one acceptable answer.	Again an emphasis is placed on the more than one right way – key to creativity and key to mathematics.
Pupils with widely differing abilities and interests were fully engaged and appropriately challenged.	If mathematics is viewed as entirely a hierarchical subject, there is an assumption that some children will be unable to undertake certain challenges. Group working and a problem-solving approach can overcome some of these difficulties. Lower-achieving children can sometimes achieve surprising results when the challenges motivate and engage them.
Teachers and pupils used many kinds of technology effectively: to gather information, to model possible solutions to complex questions, to construct presentations and to communicate in an engaging and provocative way.	Mathematical data can be presented in some exciting and innovative ways.
Role play was used to explore ideas, to encourage empathy and speculation, to practise working in teams and making decisions, and to build confidence.	MakeBelieve Arts has used role play and other drama techniques very effectively to promote mathematical understanding. Story is at the root of imaginative play and drama and has a strong part to play in developing mathematical understanding (Haven 2007). These issues will be explored in subsequent chapters.
Teachers and pupils responded enthusiastically, purposefully and with curiosity to opportunities offered by partnerships and outsiders with specific expertise.	Positive mathematical dispositions are vital in supporting mathematical understanding. Teachers and parents, in common with most other adults, are often not enthusiastic about maths and this can have a dramatic impact on children's achievement. Creative approaches can revitalise teaching – giving new routes into mathematics.

TEACHING MATHEMATICS CREATIVELY

In the chapters that follow we intend to explore a range of topics relevant to the consideration of creative mathematics. These are not offered as recipes or as the one right way to approach mathematics. Indeed that would be far from the spirit of creativity. Rather, we hope that they will enable you to see possibilities that work for you and the children you teach. Similarly, while in some cases the age of children involved is indicated, this is not intended to be taken as a definitive guide. Children vary and do not always learn according to the *ladder of rules* (Boaler 2009) which mathematics education has established. Interest and experience will often determine what children are able to do – and how they approach mathematics and learning.

Chapter 2 will consider dispositions to mathematics while Chapter 3 will focus on the problem-solving nature of mathematics. Chapter 4 explores the nature of mathematical talking and thinking. Chapter 5 examines what makes mathematics real (rather than fake) for children. There is a strong emphasis on story throughout the book, but Chapter 6 outlines some of the reasons for this as well as exploring some of the practical uses of books and story. Chapters 7 to 11 highlight different aspects of curricular provision and their role in developing mathematical understanding, while the final chapter considers the nature of creative, and therefore playful, teaching.

Throughout the book, in addition to the theme of story, an emphasis will be placed on the role of play and physical action in mathematical learning. Understanding of pattern, the use of imagination, the use of technology and the aesthetics of mathematics will be explored further. The role of cross-phase learning and teaching and the impact of an inclusive approach will be further themes.

CONCLUSION

It is apparent that radical changes are needed in the teaching of mathematics. Despite the fact that we are all born mathematical, too many adults fear and dislike mathematics – and therefore feel unable to use it in their everyday lives. Innovations in policy and practice have made some improvements but this is not enough. At the root of the difficulty lies the fact that educators have worked hard to develop practice, focusing on making mathematics more real or more concrete. While vital, this does not take account of the need to develop abstract thought (Pound 2006). Creative approaches, with their symbolic and motivational properties, help children to bridge the two. By teaching creatively teachers can support children in becoming creative learners.

FURTHER READING

Alexander, R. (ed.) (2010) *Children, Their World, Their Education*. London: Routledge.

Boaler, J. (2009) *The Elephant in the Classroom*. London: Souvenir Press.

Devlin, K. (2000) *The Maths Gene*. London: Weidenfeld and Nicolson.

Gardner, H. (2006) *Five Minds for the Future.* Boston, MA.: Harvard Business School Press.

Namy, L. L. (ed.) (2005) *Symbol Use and Symbolic Representation*. Mahwah, NJ: Lawrences Erlbaum Associates Inc.

CHILDREN'S BOOKS

Gravett, E. (2009) *The Rabbit Problem*. London: Macmillan Children's Books.

The cover blurb for this book states that it is based on the work of the thirteenth-century mathematician Fibonacci. It also states that it is not a book about maths but about rabbits. Try it out – is this maths? It's certainly creative!

CHAPTER 2

I HATE MATHS! POSITIVE FEELINGS, CREATIVE DISPOSITIONS AND MATHEMATICS

TRISHA'S STORY

As I begin writing a book for teachers on approaches to mathematics I reflect on the irony of this. At school I hated maths. By the time I was in Year 6, I was certain that I was destined never to be any good at the subject. Three of my previous teachers had been very clear about this fact. It wasn't that I didn't understand some of it; my main problem was I often rushed my sums and made what the teachers very specifically defined in red pen on all my books as careless mistakes. I fidgeted a lot at school. I got bored easily. I was easy to engage in a subject but just as easily distracted if I didn't see the point in something.

By the time we started on algebraic equations I had totally lost any interest in the subject. On a good day I would be the annoying child who asked: why are we doing this, and what good will it do me in my future life? On a bad day I would doodle on the back of my exercise book, but on very few days would I engage with the learning.

My other problem was that I didn't, and actually still don't to this day, know any more than my 2, 5 and 10 times tables without counting on my fingers. I tried to learn them, but they just didn't stick. So when times tables were introduced as short cuts, they were never any shorter for me. It was only years later as a parent struggling to teach my dyslexic 7-year-old son his times tables using as many creative and fun ways as I could think of that I realised that for some of us, this kind of information is never going to stick no matter how many bottles of shaving foam are poured onto trays to finger trace $7 \times 7 = 49$. Needless to say I failed maths obtaining a CSE Grade 3 at the end of secondary school. In my twenties I retook it so that I could do a PGCE teacher training, and I finally passed with GCSE grade C, not brilliant, but enough to count. The good thing about my experience at school was it left me with a hunger to work with children and teachers on developing approaches that support pupils in engaging with the curriculum in a way that I had never been able to.

My journey to this book has been a practical one, having read Egan's work on *Teaching as Storytelling* (1988) I became fascinated with his premise that you can teach anything through a story – *even mathematics*. Suddenly it brought back all of my experiences with maths at school. I began a journey into mathematics that has excited and enriched me. Creating stories and exercises to teach mathematics as part of my role at MakeBelieve Arts has been an exciting experience. My maths has improved along the way, but I had a purpose for learning it. I needed to understand the maths in order to find a way to make it creative. I have held algebra picnics with Year 7 pupils and giants' parties with Reception to Year 4. I have worked with pupils on creating rap songs to remember the three types of averages and I now approach maths as an exciting and dynamic subject. My primary school teachers of old would have been very surprised if they'd heard me say that all those years ago. I have become passionate about education – even (or perhaps especially) about mathematics education.

FEELINGS ABOUT MATHEMATICS

Trisha's experience is by no means unique. For many children and adults alike, mathematics is a subject that elicits strong negative reactions. Boaler (2009) reports that it is the second most disliked subject – only science is more disliked amongst schoolchildren. Adults' reactions in any discussion of the subject are often 'I hated maths' or 'my maths teacher hated me' or 'it was never my favourite subject'. Atkinson (1992) researched parents' views of mathematics – some talked of their panic and suffering while others focused on the content. One parent is reported as saying 'I don't approve of all this messing about with shapes and cubes' (Atkinson 1992: 165) and another talked of the need for doing 'real maths' – not practical stuff! Trisha's account and the anxieties of many adults (including parents) highlight a number of important misunderstandings about the nature of mathematics.

Why do feelings matter?

Negative feelings about mathematics cause disaffection or a kind of learning paralysis. The feelings Trisha describes about sitting in the class and failing to engage with the mathematical ideas on offer will be recognised by many readers. Enthusiasm and interest are what make us good learners. Trisha learnt enough maths when she needed to for her own purposes and this is often the case but she still acknowledges that there are areas where she feels she will never overcome the barriers established in childhood. Some adults talk of their inability to use mathematics in their everyday lives almost as a badge of honour – but perhaps this is just defensiveness. Others determine to get over it.

Stephen, for example, was a teaching assistant. Although studying for an honours degree in his own time, he felt that this could never be for anything other than his own interest. Tutors suggested that he might consider taking a PGCE but he felt that what he saw as his inability to do maths was an insurmountable barrier. His tutors persisted and Stephen sought the help of the university's access services. He attended a summer course to diagnose his difficulties and, like Trisha, was eventually able to successfully undertake a PGCE. Devlin (2000: 254) suggests that wanting to do maths is the key to success – 'when people find that they really need to master some mathematics, they invariably do so'.

A range of neuroscientific evidence (Goleman 1996; Gerhardt 2004; LeDoux 1998) has underlined the impact of feelings and emotions on learning. LeDoux, for example, describes in some detail the way in which conditioned fear responses arise. They may arise after only one incident; they may be reawakened by something apparently unrelated; may be unconscious and in some cases very long-lasting. Transfer this idea from rats to the maths classes that many adults attended, and you begin to see why so many members of the population hold such negative feelings about the subject.

Although adults can get over a negative disposition towards mathematics, those working with children should aim to avoid setting up such feelings in the first place. Positive learning dispositions such as curiosity, perseverance and persistence, making unusual connections, confidence and communication underpin successful learning across the curriculum (Pound 2006). Adults need to support and maintain positive dispositions in their teaching of mathematics. Throughout this book, the focus will be on teaching which engages children, which promotes effective communication and boosts rather than undermines confidence.

The attitudes we communicate to children influence heavily the way they view mathematics. The parents that Atkinson (1992: 165) interviewed made constant references to their own experience, saying things such as:

> Most of all I don't want them to panic like I did . . .
>
> I wasn't any good at maths so I don't suppose my child will be either . . .
>
> I don't want my child to suffer what I went through. I want her to enjoy it and understand it.

Paradoxically, there are also parents who failed at maths at school and want their children to do better, yet still feel that the teaching their children undergo should be like that which they themselves endured unsuccessfully (Pound 2006). The attitude which adults display, whether parents, teachers or support staff, has an impact on children. We owe it to them to do all that we can – as Trisha did – to develop our own enthusiasm and, in the process, our expertise.

A potential area of conflict arises from the differing views of staff and parents about what counts as maths. It is this difference which contributes to children's feeling that if they haven't been sitting at a table with a pencil in their hand, they have not been doing real maths. This is a vital aspect when considering how to set about teaching mathematics creatively. Teachers and support staff need to keep parents informed about the approaches to mathematics they are using and why. This may involve workshops, handouts, displays and speakers but it will certainly involve a lot of talk. The job of staff will be made very much easier where there is a whole-school approach and clear policy. If you want to teach mathematics successfully through story or dance or drama you will need to prepare parents (and probably some of the staff you are working with). Children will sense differences of opinion and will value these potentially rich opportunities less.

Do we need to be accurate?

Most of the mathematics that we use in our everyday lives relies on guesswork and approximations. We estimate how much our shopping will cost, how much milk we'll need between now and next Thursday, whether we've got time to have a bath before we go out, or how many rolls of wallpaper we will need. Some calculations are required but there is usually a significant amount of leeway. Of course there are situations where absolute accuracy is required. In preparing for space travel, for example, it is a matter of life and death, but in most everyday situations it is not. Where it is important calculators and computers can help us to achieve accuracy – providing we have a rough idea of what the answer should be.

Devlin (2000) makes the point that the human brain is good at estimating but much less good at accurate calculations. He suggests that the difficulties faced by Trisha (and others) in learning tables, for example, stem from the brain's enjoyment of pattern and the way in which our memories work by association. We actively look for patterns, even where none is obvious and we try to connect everything since this is how we make it memorable. Although by the age of seven, several two-digit number bonds are well established, as multiplication tables are introduced, children begin to make apparently careless errors. He argues that children who previously confidently knew that $2 + 3 = 5$ may begin to say that $2 + 3 = 6$ but rarely that $2 + 3 = 7$. The numbers associated with addition and multiplication begin to interfere with one another. He gives a further example where the interference comes from language itself:

> asked for 5×6 . . . [we] answer 36 or 56. Somehow, reading the 5 and the 6 brings to mind both incorrect answers. People do not make such errors as $2 \times 3 = 23$ or $3 \times 7 = 37$. Because the numbers 23 and 37 do not appear in *any* multiplication table, our associative memory does not bring them up in the context of multiplication. But 36 and 56 are both in the table, so when our brain sees 5×6, both are activated.
>
> (Devlin 2000: 63)

To sum up, our brains have excellent survival skills of seeking out patterns, making connections and making rapid judgements or guesses. These enable us to make decisions quickly and on the basis of relatively little information. They form the basis of what is sometimes called intuition (Claxton 2000). For Claxton, intuition is one of the many 'ways of knowing' employed by humans and involves expertise (which may be unreflective or unconscious), judgement, and awareness or sensitivity. He further suggests that it includes 'rumination' or 'chewing the cud' (Claxton 2000: 40) and creativity. Creativity, he claims, requires reflection – one of the components of creativity put forward in the NACCCE report (1999).

Schiro (2004: 57), whose writing considers the role of narrative in mathematics education at all stages and phases, suggests that the role of the teacher is to:

> help children know mathematics on the intuitive level where 'they know it in their bones'. Once they have an intuitive understanding of and feel for mathematics, then they can move on to understand it at a more abstract, generalised objective level.

This is not an approach confined to children. Claxton (cited in Alexander 2010: 274) reminds us that real mathematicians do not operate in the inflexible way indicated by so many approaches to mathematics teaching and learning. Devlin underlines this view by refuting the myth that mathematicians use logic as their starting point. Once they have an idea (or hypothesis) they use logic and reasoning to arrive at a means of proving (or disproving) their initial idea. He writes:

> Precise, formal reasoning is not required for mathematical discovery. Rather its purposes are verification of things already discovered (or perhaps suspected) . . . The need for formal verification is a direct consequence of the nature of mathematical discovery (which includes) trial and error, guesswork, intuition, and conversation with others.
>
> (Devlin 2000: 252)

Getting things right, or being accurate, on the other hand, makes different demands on our brains – as Devlin and Claxton's views indicate. In teaching mathematics we place the emphasis on accuracy – the thing our brains find hardest. At the same time, we often underplay the aspects of thinking, including mathematical thinking that we are good at. Too often, we tell children not to guess – but guessing comes naturally and has to be the starting point for all thinking. As we guess, the brain begins to explore possible connections.

We have many 'ways of knowing' and approaches to teaching mathematics should exploit them all. Devlin (2000) suggests, for example, that multiplication tables are best learnt through sound patterns – the very technique that Trisha used with her son. Raps, songs, chants will all support children in committing the facts to memory. Have you noticed how even very fluent users of a second language will often revert to their home or first language when making mathematical computations? Devlin (2000: 63) suggests that this is because:

> no matter how fluent they become in their second language . . . it's easier to slip back into their first language to calculate and then to translate the result back, than to try to relearn the multiplication table in their second language.

CHANGING MINDS AND FEELINGS

In order to develop creative approaches to mathematics the attitudes, minds (and hearts) of many parents, teachers and support staff will have to be changed. Deeply held views of what maths is and how it ought to be taught have to be challenged. In this section four key aspects of changing minds and feelings are explored:

- gaining insight into the complex nature of mathematics
- gaining insight into the complex nature of children's learning
- engendering enthusiasm and excitement
- developing whole-school approaches.

The complex nature of mathematics

One important way of changing minds is to raise adults' awareness of just what a complex process number, for example, is. In order for you to get a taste of this, Table 2.1 shows a nursery rhyme, *The Grand Old Duke of York*, set out as a counting

Table 2.1 Is maths hard? An activity based on *The Grand Old Duke of York*

The Grand Old Duke of York

The	Grand	Old	Duke	of	York				
1	2	3	4	5	6				
He	had	ten	thousand	men					
7	8	9	10	11					
He	marched	them	up	to	the	top	of	the	hill
12	13	14	15	16	17	18	19	20	21
And	he	marched	them	down	again				
22	23	24	25	26	27				
And	when	they	were	up	they	were	up		
28	29	30	31	32	33	34	35		
And	when	they	were	down	they	were	down		
36	37	38	39	40	41	42	43		
And	when	they	were	only	halfway	up			
44	45	46	47	48	49	50			
They	were	neither	up	nor	down.				
51	52	53	54	55	56				

Try these 'sums' at first without looking at the key provided.
Here is an example:

- had + ten = the

Now try these:

- thousand + men =?
- marched − York = ? or ?
- hill divided by Old = ?
- top × Old = ?

system. There are also some suggestions of sums and counting activities for you to try. Although this is an artificial example and it doesn't bear much similarity to the counting system we use, there are some important parallels:

- Simply knowing the number names in order does not make it easy to pick out a single number word without starting again at the beginning.
- There are some confusions. In this instance the confusion could be related to the fact that there is more than one he or hill. For children the confusion may be about the fact that 2 and 5 look somewhat similar.
- Associations or unwonted connections can get in the way of understanding. In this rhyme, thousand = 10 and ten = 9. For children the associations may be about the fact that gran's house number is 14 while the bus they go to the shops on is 44.

The complex nature of learning

Another important way of changing minds and feelings is to raise awareness of the learning that is occurring in interesting and challenging situations. Two published stories of children's struggle with mathematical concepts underline what adults can learn from observing and reflecting on children's actions and comments. The first story involves five- and six-year-old children in an Italian nursery in Reggio Emilia – a region of the country which it has been claimed has some of the best early childhood education in the world. A group of children was invited to design a table which a carpenter would then construct. Castagnetti and Vecchi (1997) describe and illustrate the processes involved for adults and children. They describe the way in which adults observed and reflected on what they saw children doing and suggest that collecting what they term 'documentation' of this sort 'gives new strength to the "potential genius" of teachers . . . giving freedom and meaning to a job that is too often humiliated and fraught with routine' (Castagnetti and Vecchi 1997: 13).

The second story involves a group of American children, aged five (Paley 1981). They too are involved in an activity which involves measurement – but of a rather different nature. Two children are about to act out the story of Jack and the Beanstalk. They have two rugs but one child believes that one is bigger than the other and that it should therefore represent the giant's castle rather than Jack's house while the other child believes them to be of the same size. They and a group of friends undertake a number of initiatives in order to establish which is larger.

What links these two stories is the children's view of standard measurement. In both cases rulers are introduced by adults but rejected by the children. Both groups of children move back and forth between using standard and non-standard measurements. Interestingly the Italian group make their own metre sticks – which are of course non-standard. The approach of the teachers in the two stories is somewhat different – Vivian Gussin Paley takes it upon herself to remind the children about the set of rulers and the steel tape measure but in the eyes of the children these are not 'real'. The children designing a table introduce the idea of standard measurement for themselves. Rinaldi (writing in Castagnetti and Vecchi 1997: 103) discusses the issue of whether or not the role of the teacher is to produce relevant tools at the exact moment at which children might want them. She writes:

> The real problem, then, is not when and how to explain or present standard measuring instruments to children (at what age? in what way?), but rather to ask how can we create the conditions that enable the development of divergent and creative thought; how to sustain the ability and the pleasure involved in comparing ideas with others rather than simply confronting a single idea that is presumed to be 'true' or 'right' . . .

The school and the classroom become the place where each individual is confronted with the need to explain his own knowledge – first of all to himself – in order to compare it, loan it, exchange it with others. This requires the teacher to be inside the context, fully participating, above all because she is curious to understand the various ways that children observe, interpret, and represent the world . . .

The path of learning that children and adults construct together originates from these ways and worlds represented by each child. We construct not only knowledge but also an awareness of how this construction takes place: exchange, dialogue, divergence, negotiation, and also the pleasure of thinking and working together.

Both stories illustrate the way in which children are in, what Vivian Gussin Paley has described as, 'temporary custody' of mathematical concepts. They vacillate between apparent complex understandings and complete denial of what appear to adults to be facts. Tommaso, for example, measures the base of the leg of the table by saying 'It's half of half of half of the shoe' (Castagnetti and Vecchi 1997: 71) – a remarkable insight. Wally and his friends have found a way to measure the rugs which involves using children. Paley (1981), as teacher, asks the children whether they could measure the rugs in a way which didn't rely on people being tall or short. They try rulers but refuse to accept that the same ruler might be used more than once – since it leaves gaps. They use a steel tape but 156 has little meaning – measurement only comes to life the next day when Warren, just the right size to be a rug-measurer, returns to school. Castagnetti and Vecchi (1997: 49) reflect on the fascinating way in which children learn complex ideas:

> Children's routes are often unpredictable, at least to us. They do not always follow a linear and consistent path, in either action or thought. They construct, lose, detour, or temporarily abandon their schemas, abstraction, and strategies. We adults have to be prepared for surprises.

This unpredictablility (and the surprises it brings to the teacher) is not confined to children. A group of student teachers in training (all of whom were required to have a minimum of grade C at GCSE) were exploring place value involving hundreds, tens and units. They were cutting up squared paper to represent three-digit numbers. Far from finding this a childish activity, one student in particular became very animated and exclaimed, 'I've done so many sums and just never realised that this is what I was doing! Now I know what it looks like.'

Engendering enthusiasm and excitement

One of the reasons for teaching mathematics creatively is to ensure that the subject does not become boring. Excitement and exuberance, or what Egan (1991) calls 'ecstatic responses', support learning and memory, by altering the chemistry of the brain (Eliot 1999). This in turn makes learning more effective. Boredom and disaffection stultify learning while excitement, though hard to manage, is a means of enhancing engagement and enthusiasm for the subject.

Adopting the range of creative approaches to the teaching of mathematics outlined in this book will help to show children what an exciting area of learning mathematics can be. Music, dance and physical action all enhance enjoyment. While enjoying mathematics is undoubtedly not enough, it is a necessary preliminary to becoming good at it. Research into the nature of genius (Howe 1999) has famously demonstrated the way in which engagement is the key to mastery. It is estimated that in order to become very good at anything one must practise for ten thousand hours. In order to put in ten thousand hours one must really want to do something! If we want children to become good at mathematics, we need to make the subject sufficiently interesting that children want to spend time doing it.

One aspect of human behaviour which always engenders excitement is story. As Trish's account (at the beginning of this chapter) of her difficulties with mathematics while at school points out, it was Egan's challenge that anything, *even maths*, can be taught through story. Simply say to a group of adults (or children) that you are going to tell them a story and they relax into comfortable listening mode. Devlin (2000) points out:

a The human mind loves story and can cope with complex and abstract ideas in stories, such as soap operas, because the context is familiar.

b Not only can we cope with these stories but we love them so much that overall, two-thirds of all human interaction is made up of gossip, chat, narrative. If late for a meeting, we rarely just apologise, we like to tell the story! 'The dog ate my homework and then was sick on the baby!' 'A hamster ran under the bus!' 'The road was flooded, the bus skidded, my bottle of water poured into the man's hat and the bus driver stopped for a pint at the pub!'

c What real mathematicians do is to enter a world of mathematics – which he suggests 'requires considerable conscious effort to train the mind to follow the soap opera we call mathematics' (Devlin 2000: 257). He continues: 'mathematics becomes possible for the mathematician because she spends sufficient time in the abstract world of mathematics for it to achieve a degree of reality for her. But whereas the real world constantly reinforces the abstract world of the television soap opera, the mathematician herself must provide that reinforcement for the mathematical soap opera.'

Developing whole-school approaches

Teaching mathematics creatively needs to be adopted throughout the school. Confining it to the early years gives the message that playfulness and enjoyment are something

TEACHERS' ENTHUSIASM AND EXCITEMENT

Five groups of teachers, on a training course, were set the problem of dividing irregularly shaped islands equally into eight parts. The task was meant to be completed in 10 minutes. Prior to the INSET we had marked out the islands on the floor in masking tape in an ad-hoc fashion. One group of teachers had metre sticks, unifix cubes and spare masking tape as the tools they could use to make their calculations. What we hadn't factored in was that the island was drawn out on a parquet floor. The teachers ingeniously used this factor in their calculations and began placing unfix cubes on every section of the flooring. They then began counting the cubes to work out how many sections of wood there were so that they could divide these into 8 equal parts. Once this was done they started marking out accurately on the floor the division between each of the sections following along the lines of the parquet pattern.

By this time we had begun calling the groups back to report on their process. We realised that this group were reluctant to leave what they had started and all of us gathered around their island where they explained their idea. The group of five teachers were so engaged in their task that they found it difficult to leave the work unfinished. How fantastic it would be if in our maths lessons we were able to provoke such meticulous focus as this one activity engendered during an early morning INSET on the second day of January.

to be grown out of, while confining it to the later years indicates that you must have a certain level of knowledge before you can be creative. This has the disadvantage that children are likely to have been turned off mathematics before ever finding out about any of its engaging features. Both are major disadvantages in developing a culture of strong mathematical thinking and understanding.

As Bruner's theories (1986) demonstrate, enactive learning is the starting point for all new learning and as Moyle's play spiral (1989) underlines, new learning constantly occurs in familiar contexts. Creative approaches to mathematics involving narrative, music, drama, physical action, dance, can be used effectively throughout the primary school and on into the secondary school (see Schiro 2004). This view of learning is often linked to learning styles and multiple intelligence theories (Gardner 1999) but it is broader in concept. It will be explored further throughout this book.

Exploratory play is readily identified as being connected to problem-solving but imaginative play is all too rarely identified in schools as being part of that process. Long-standing research (Sylva *et al.* 1976) and more recent research (Devlin 2000) have made important links between children's imaginative play and their ability to think conjecturally – an important aspect of problem-solving. This theme will be developed further, particularly in the next chapter.

A further aspect of whole-school development of creative approaches to the teaching and learning of mathematics is the role of teachers in giving 'permission' for children to be creative. They will best do this by being creative themselves. Cremin (2010: 4) describes creative teachers as giving 'high value to curiosity and risk taking, to ownership, autonomy and making connections' in their pupils. Moreover they regard 'the development of imaginative and unusual ideas in both themselves and their students' as being important. She goes on to suggest that 'whilst all good teachers reward originality, creative ones depend on it to enhance their own wellbeing and that of the children'.

CONCLUSION

Boaler (2009) describes the high level of negative emotions about maths amongst adults and children, and the poor standards achieved by so many, and argues that living and working in today's world requires much greater mathematical abilities. She also comments on the negative view of mathematics which is so often depicted in popular media and contrasts this with the obvious pleasure that so many people find in the logical and mathematical thinking involved in sudokus, kakuros and so on. She continues:

> There are two versions of maths in the lives of many people: the strange and boring subject that they encountered in classrooms and an interesting set of ideas that is the maths of the world, and is curiously different and surprisingly engaging.
>
> (Boaler 2009: 7)

The focus of the chapters that follow is an attempt to draw those two worlds of mathematics closer together – recognising the creative nature of the subject and teaching it through what Boaler calls 'a problem-solving approach'.

FURTHER READING

Devlin, K. (2000) *The Maths Gene*. London: Weidenfeld and Nicolson (see Chapter 3, 'Everybody counts').

Paley, V. G. (1981) *Wally's Stories*. London: Harvard University Press.

Singh, S. (1997) *Fermat's Last Theorem*. London: Fourth Estate.

CHILDREN'S BOOKS

Agard, J. (2003) *Einstein: The Girl who Hated Maths*. London: Hodder Children's Books.
Copyright prevents us quoting from this wonderful book. It's full of great ideas about the world of mathematics. Buy it and recite the poems – you won't regret it!

CHAPTER 3 MOTIVATING CHILDREN: PROBLEM FINDING AND PROBLEM SOLVING

To suggest that problem solving lies at the heart of mathematics is often to produce a deep sigh in many people. Adult memories of their schooling almost always include dealing with maths problems which might have been purely computational – rows of fractions, for example, just waiting to have the right answer attached, or written problems with a lot of text and the need to identify the correct strategy or algorithm, previously taught by the teacher. Boaler (2009: 38) challenges this approach to problem solving:

> Children begin school as natural problem-solvers and many studies have shown that students are better at solving problems before they attend maths classes. They think and reason their way through problems, using methods in creative ways, but after a few hundred hours of passive maths learning students have their problem solving abilities knocked out of them.

FIRST FIND THE PROBLEM!

> Problem solving is natural to young children because the world is new to them, and they exhibit curiosity, intelligence, and flexibility as they face new situations. The challenge at this level is to build on children's innate problem-solving inclinations and to preserve and encourage a disposition that values problem-solving.
>
> (NCTM 2000: item 116)

Mathematics is actually about raising questions as much as it is about solving them. The ability to shape (or ask) and to solve mathematical problems is the essence of constructing mathematical meaning. Adults can help to pose problems which engage pupils and mean that they have to find mathematical solutions, giving real understanding and purpose to a maths lesson. But problem finding helps children to become enthusiastic about problems. In this way they also develop the sound learning dispositions which will support problem solving throughout life and across subjects. Just as when babies are learning to talk, adults work from their utterances (see for example Whitehead 2009), so in mathematics it appears to be beneficial to work from children's own problems (Pound 2006).

Counting on Frank (Clement 1995) epitomises the problem-seeking view of a curious 8-year-old. The hero imagines how many of his dog Frank it would take to fill the house; he imagines himself putting on all his clothes – starting with the smallest items and working through to the bulkiest. He estimates that had he (accidentally?) knocked 15 of the hated peas off his plate every day throughout his life, they would now be level with the table top. This, he declares, would have the added benefit of letting his mother know that he doesn't like peas!

Humans are born problem seekers. Babies and toddlers will work tirelessly to solve problems of their own choosing. Gopnik *et al.* (1999: 163), citing the seventeenth-century philosopher Hobbes, describe our drive to seek and solve problems as 'a lust of the mind'. They suggest that:

> we look beyond the surfaces of the world and try to infer its deeper patterns. We look for the underlying, hidden causes of events. We try to figure out the nature of things.
>
> It's not just that we humans *can* do this; we *need* to do it. . . . When we're presented with a puzzle, a mystery, a hint of a pattern, something that doesn't quite make sense, we work until we find a solution. In fact, we intentionally set ourselves such problems . . . like crossword puzzles, video games or detective stories.
>
> (Gopnik *et al.* 1999: 85)

AN ASIDE ABOUT HUMOUR AND MATHEMATICS

Children, in fact adults too, learn through humour (Meek 1992; Egan 1991) and humour is an important element of creative thinking. It is also an important aspect of problem solving – thinking of every possible solution including the apparently ridiculous ones. Yet we tend to think that mathematics is not a laughing matter. Out-moded behaviourist thinking leads us to worry that if we stray from right answers into jokes, incorrect answers will somehow become burnished on to the brain, never to be eradicated. On the contrary, joking allows us to explore uncertainties and establish the boundaries between reality and unreality, encouraging us to engage in reflective thinking. At the risk of being thought to be 'giving peas a chance', in addition to *Counting on Frank*, *Eat your peas* (Gray and Sharratt 2001) also deserves a mention. It includes some straightforward counting, such as ten chocolate factories, but it also offers some huge but imaginary quantities such as a 'gazillionpillionwillion'. Moreover it involves some interesting negotiation as when Daisy offers, despite all the bribes offered by mum, to eat her peas if her mother will eat *her* brussel sprouts. Mathematical thinking (and joking) on every page!

Papert, designer of Logo, is described on his own website (http://www.papert.org) as being the 'world's foremost expert on how technology can provide new ways to learn' and as participating in 'developing the most influential cutting-edge opportunities for children to participate in the digital world'. Steeped as he has been over many decades in the uses of technology in education, he has not lost his interest in what makes children learners. He describes a conversation between two young children being introduced to working in a computer room. One is emerging from the experience; the other waiting his turn:

> 'What was it like?' The friend replied, 'It was fun.' Then paused and added: 'It was really hard.' The relation between 'fun' and 'hard' may need some interpretation. Did this mean 'it was fun in spite of being hard' or 'it was fun because it was hard'? The teacher who heard the tone of the conversation and knew the children had no doubt. The child meant it was 'fun' because it was 'hard'. It was 'hard' and this made it all the more 'fun'. Since then I have listened to children with an ear sensitised by this experience and have come to know that the concept of *hard fun* is widely present in children's thinking.
>
> (Papert 1996: 53)

Although he had worked with Piaget for some time, Papert is open to the idea that we should not put a developmental ceiling on children's understanding. Discussing Papert's work, Andrews and Trafton (2002) suggest that teachers often feel that 'keeping it simple' by limiting the problems presented to children is most likely to be effective. They identify, however, a 'shift in our view of young children from fragile learners to robust thinkers' (Andrews and Trafton 2002: 4) which should lead us to change both the pedagogy we employ and the learning environment we create.

This idea of 'hard fun' is echoed in the words of older students and mathematicians too. An adolescent evaluating a summer programme describes it as both harder and 'funner' (Boaler 2009: 1534) than his normal school work. He explains:

> In our [regular] class they give us, like, easy problems and all that. And in this class you give us hard problems to figure out. You have to figure out the pattern and all that . . . We stay on it longer . . . so we can really get to know how to do pattern blocks and everything.

Boaler (2009: 25) also reports an interview with a professor of mathematics. A question about what she found the most difficult aspect of her work was followed by one asking what was the most fun. To both questions she replied 'Trying to prove theorems'. Katz, in her foreword to *Little Kids – Powerful Problem-solvers* (Andrews and Trafton 2002), highlights as important aspects of being a problem-solver the notions of

- *hard fun*, and
- working within a community of learners.

She identifies what she believes to be important themes in maintaining and developing children's innate ability and interest in solving problems. She suggests that key to this process is:

- believing in children's competence
- supporting the development of learning dispositions such as curiosity and perseverance
- developing of mathematical competences such as estimating, predicting, hypothesising and analysing.

Some imposed mathematical problems do not engage children because they are not real. Other problems do not engage learners because they are too simple. Even newborn babies can be shown to be interested in complex problems, rather than those that are solved too easily (Bower 1977). Resnick (1988: 38) writes:

> If we are to engage students in contextualised mathematics problem solving, we must find ways to create in the classroom situations of sufficient complexity and engagement that they become mathematically engaging contexts in their own right . . . They should also permit students to develop questions, not only solve problems posed by others.

One of the important and interesting things about these problems is that they demonstrate conjectural thinking. No-one knows how tall the boy in *Counting on Frank* would be if he had grown at the same rate as the tree in his garden – there is no right or wrong answer. Conjectural thinking is an important element of creative thinking (Craft 2005) and it involves 'what if' or 'as if' thinking. Boaler (2009) describes a summer project in which a boy called Alonzo was working on a given problem. Using Multilink, children had been asked to build a staircase in order to begin to predict how many cubes would be needed to build a staircase 10 cubes high or even 100 cubes high. She noticed that:

> Alonzo seemed to be playing with the linking cubes and not working on the problem. Drawing near, we saw that Alonzo had decided to modify his staircase so that it extended in four directions. Thus a 1-block high staircase had a total of five blocks, a 2-block staircase had a total of fourteen blocks and so on. What had looked like messing around was in fact Alonzo's creativity and curiosity conspiring to produce a problem that was more diagrammatically and algebraically involved than the one that had been originally presented to him.
>
> (Boaler 2009: 160)

So impressed with Alonzo's problem-finding was she, that the teacher phoned his home to report his achievements. The mother reported that Alonzo had consistently failed his maths tests at school and that no one there had noticed his mathematical creativity. She went on to describe a project he had undertaken at home – inventing a light switch that he could operate without getting out of bed – involving just the right number of coins to operate the switch without breaking the dental floss.

LOST IN *MATHSLAND*

Some of the written problems with which we were confronted at school purported to have a story attached to them – perhaps men digging holes or pipes filling swimming pools. Boaler (2009: 45) describes problems of this sort as taking you to *Mathsland*, where 'you leave your common sense at the door' and:

> people paint houses at identical speeds all day long; [w]ater fills baths at the same rate each minute, and people run around tracks at the same distance from the edge. To do well in maths class, children know that they have to suspend reality and accept the ridiculous problems they are given. They know that if they think about the problems and use what they understand from life then they will fail.

Resnick (1988: 4) calls into question the idea behind such problems which is that mathematics is a 'well-structured discipline'. She writes that:

> Mathematics is regarded as a field in which statements have unambiguous meanings, there is a clear hierarchy of knowledge, and the range of possible actions in response to any problem is both restricted and well defined in advance . . . Educators typically treat mathematics as a field with no open questions and no arguments, at least none that young students or those not particularly talented in mathematics can appreciate . . . Even when we teach problem solving, we often present stereotyped problems and look for rules that students can use to decide what the right interpretation of the problem is – so that they can find the single appropriate answer.

She argues for the need to present mathematics as 'an ill-structured discipline' with no single answer or interpretation. This she suggests is what real mathematicians do and, further, that in order to develop mathematical thinking in children, teachers should be aiming to 'develop both capability and disposition for finding relationships among mathematical entities and between mathematical statements and situations involving quantities, relationships and patterns' (Resnick 1988: 5–6).

One step towards a more 'ill-structured' approach is to introduce problem solving earlier. Fuson (2004) argues that all too often computation involving whole numbers is taught first and then some applications (or problems) are presented. This, she suggests, can mean that less able (or less motivated) children never have the opportunity to apply their learning to any real-life (or even *Mathsland*) situations. Moreover, canny children may notice that the problems they are given are related to the sums they have just been doing and therefore may not even bother to read the problem. This results in the all too familiar situation of children asking questions at a later stage such as 'is this an add or a take-away?' In other words – 'don't bother me with having to think, just tell me how to get it right'. Fuson (2004: 116–17) cites research which indicates that:

> beginning with problem situations yields higher problem-solving competence and equal or better computational competence. Children who start with problem

situations directly model solutions to these problems. They later move on to more advanced mathematical approaches as they move through levels of solutions and of problem difficulty. Thus, the development of computational fluency and problem-solving is intertwined when both are co-developing with understanding.

STORY MATHS

The phrase 'story maths' is widely used but frequently does not involve a real story. What constitutes a real story will be considered in Chapter 6 more fully but at this stage suffice to say that three sweets shared by four children is *not* a story (nor much of a sweet). In this section we simply consider the role of stories in developing the conjectural abilities which underpin problem solving. Alonzo's conjectural thinking described earlier in this chapter is precisely the kind of thinking creative teachers want, and mathematicians would argue, ought to develop in children.

Mr Archimedes' Bath (Allen 1994), like other books by the same author (see for example *Who Sank the Boat?*), is a story of problem solving. The case study shown here involved children in a reception class who had enormous fun displacing the soft play balls in a babies' bath. Their mathematical focus was perhaps on counting – although their broader focus was certainly around scientific knowledge and understanding (DfES 2007). This highlights some important aspects of problem solving and finding – first that it is a generic skill. While there may be some aspects which are specific to mathematics, there are many others which may be learnt in a number of contexts. Second, problem solving requires rich experience. All of us solve problems by drawing on what we learned in different but similar situations. Most children will be familiar with the water in the bath rising – play contexts enable them to begin to generalise and abstract, to discuss and reflect, to rehearse and test ideas.

The example shown below was developed with a Year 2 class but in fact has plenty of potential for work with older children. A small amount of research shows that no centipede has an even number of pairs of legs, so 50 pairs and therefore 100 legs is an impossibility. However the centipede in Tony Ross' story has 42 legs, that is 21 pairs. Apparently centipedes may have less than 20 or over 300 pairs of legs! Just imagine the problem-solving or investigative possibilities those numbers open up.

Table 3.1 highlights some other stories that present problem-solving opportunities (full details of books may be found at the end of this chapter). Story-lines can be developed without reference to a particular book – the published book can simply be regarded as a starting point. *Moon Jump a Cowntdown* (Brown 1993), sadly out of print, provides a good example as just such a starting point. It essentially asks 'how did the cow (in *Hey Diddle Diddle*) jump over the moon?' In the book, 10 cows variously try a trapeze, a pogo stick, a diving board and so on. Actually children's (and adults') own creative responses are at least as good as those provided by the author. The starting point is the question which does not, and cannot, have a right answer.

MATHS FOCUS *MR ARCHIMEDES' BATH*

- Problem solving
- Measures
- Looking for patterns and explanations

Scenario

Archimedes shares his bath with a kangaroo, a wombat and a goat, but he realises that after every time they have a bath there is water left on the floor. He decides to find who out the culprit is. Using a stick to measure the changes in water level, Archimedes and the animals take turns getting in and out of the bath to begin to discover their answer.

Exploration

1. Using coloured water, children explored how high the water level rose when they placed in differently sized and weighted objects. They discussed which object pushed the water level up the furthest.
2. A baby bath filled with soft balls was used to examine how many balls came out when children and adults of different sizes sat in the bath. They explored whether the number of balls that came out would be greater or smaller depending on the size of the person sitting down.

Outcomes

- The children greatly enjoyed the realisation that more balls were pushed out of the bath when an adult sat inside, than when one of their peers sat down.

Quotes from evaluation

> The children enjoyed exploring this maths topic in such a fun way. At the beginning of the lesson they expected the results to be the opposite to what they were, heavier people pushing out fewer balls. The value for them of having a chance to test their theories really embedded the learning.
>
> Reception class teacher

Further information

Although MakeBelieve Arts' work with this book was with children of reception age, using water, weights and ball pools to explore the subsequent maths topics that this story opens up has the potential to span a much larger age group.

Reference

Allen, P. (1994) *Mr Archimedes' Bath.* London: Picture Puffins.

http://www.mathsonline.co.uk/nonmembers/gamesroom/sims/archi/archi4.html – in this online programme you can watch a bath filling and see how much difference is made when Archimedes jumps in. The programme includes a graph that is created online to measure water height versus time depending on the tap being turned on or off and the plug being in or out.

MATHS FOCUS *CENTIPEDE'S 100 SHOES*

- Problem-solving
- Multiplication
- Division
- Addition
- Subtraction
- Directional and positional language
- Pattern

Scenario

A centipede falls over and hurts himself; to stop this happening again he buys 100 shoes to protect his feet. Once he tries them on he discovers that he has far too many shoes left over – the centipede only had 42 legs. Next he realises that the shoes rub and make his feet sore, so he asks his aunties to knit him 42 socks. Finally, frustrated at the length of time it takes to put on the 42 pairs of shoes and socks each day, he decides to distribute them between all his other insect friends. He has to work out how many legs they each have and makes sure they all get something to keep them warm.

Exploration

1. Twenty-one children were invited to wear 42 large adult socks over their shoes to form a giant centipede that marched around the classroom. Instructions were called out to remind the centipede which foot it should be using first. Other directional and positional language was incorporated, number of paces forward, backwards, to the sides etc. Other children in the class took turns to instruct the centipede as well as swapping in so they all could experience what it was like to co-ordinate such a long body.
2. Cut-out socks and shoes were given to the children to divide between a range of cut-out spiders, ants, woodlice and bees. The instructions were that every insect needed something to keep them warm, but that there was no right or wrong way to do this. Some children worked with a large collection of plastic spiders, ladybirds, worms etc. to determine how the socks could be shared out.
3. Groups of children sitting back to back explored how many of the group needed to hold out a leg or an arm to make up the correct number of legs for various insects.

Outcomes

- The maths exercise had an additional unexpected outcome in that it resulted in the class having to find a way to work together as a team in order to co-ordinate the process of walking as a giant centipede.
- This team work carried on into the group work, where the children had to support each other to make sure they held out the correct number of legs and arms to make the insects.

continued . . .

MATHS FOCUS ***CENTIPEDE'S 100 SHOES*** . . . *continued*

Quotes from evaluation

> The extent of the maths and cross curricular work we covered in this programme was greater than we originally anticipated. The children became fascinated with the patterns they could create distributing socks and shoes to the various insects. Knowing there was no right or wrong answer in this exercise felt really liberating for the group.
>
> MakeBelieve Arts workshop leader

Further information

The work arising from this story was developed by MakeBelieve Arts for a Year 2 class but it has the potential for work with both older and younger children.

References

Ross, T. (2002) *Centipede's 100 Shoes*. London: Andersen Press Ltd.

STRATEGIES

Although we are born problem-finders, our inclination and ability to seek and solve problems is dependent on the experiences we have and the strategies we develop. The apparently endless play, exploration and rehearsal which young children engage in is their way of reflecting on and storing information about their experiences (Eliot 1999). Strategies are based on previous experience – both successful and unsuccessful – in solving the problems that engage us. There are a number of significant features in the development of problem-solving strategies:

- *Play:* play and exploration are vital elements. One of the striking features of the description of Alonzo's investigation is the teacher's use of the phrase 'messing about'. Exploration often looks like messing about but seems to be an important factor – examining the limits between reality and non-reality; taking risks without serious consequences.
- *Reasoning*: this is generally thought of as involving logic but as will become clear as you read this book, mathematics is not all about logic. Reasoning will almost certainly involve pattern identification since mathematics is the science of pattern and humans are born pattern-seekers. Reasoning may also be described in terms of the identification of relationships, sequences, discussion and representations (National Strategies 2006).
- *Representing*: thinking and explaining mathematically generally leads us to represent our ideas in some way. This may be no more than counting on our fingers or describing our idea but it may involve complex arrays of figures, scribbled diagrams, graphs or models. Representing ideas visually, orally (or even aurally) gives opportunities to explore, refine and modify ideas. Boaler (2009)

Table 3.1 Stories with problem-solving opportunities

Title of book	Synopsis	Possibilities
Snail's Birthday Wish (Rempt and Smit 2006)	Snail can never keep up with his friends so he wants a car. For his birthday each of his friends presents him with a mysterious object or set of objects. At the end his friends solve the mystery by building a car from the materials they have given him.	Children could *either* work from a finished present to determine what components could be presented *or* groups of children could be given sets of components and asked to produce a present.
One is a Snail, Ten is a Crab (Sayre and Sayre 2006)	Although this is essentially just a counting book, it is one which could be used by any class in the primary school. In fact one school used it as a whole-school topic. It is subtitled 'a counting by feet book'.	This is the starting point for mathematics at many levels: simple counting; odds and evens; multiplication; division. Children may work with toy dogs, snails etc. or develop other symbols to represent the creatures in the book. Endless questions such as 'how many different ways can you represent fifty or sixty?' are possible. It might also awaken other interests, for example one is a monocycle; two is a bike; three is a trike and so on.
A New House for Mouse (Horacek 2004)	Mouse finds an apple too big to fit into his house. While searching for a bigger house he begins to eat the apple and eventually returns to his own house in which the apple will now fit easily.	A joy with young children – try acting it out with them wearing a rucksack stuffed full. Gradually removing items means that they can fit into smaller and smaller spaces.
Ouch! (Scammell and Terry 2006)	A hedgehog gets an apple stuck on his prickles. The strategies he tries to remove the apple only mean that he ends up with more and more things stuck to his back until a goat comes along and eats the items stuck on his back.	This presents many opportunities for discussing problem-solving strategies. What else could hedgehog try to do in order to get rid of the items on his prickles?
The Great Pet Sale (Inkpen 1998)	A variety of odd, and in some cases damaged, pets are on sale at knock-down prices. The hero works out that for £1 he can buy everything in the shop. The creative twist in the tale is that it is all too easy to jump to the conclusion that the author's got his sums wrong. Look carefully to find the trap in both this and in *Centipede's 100 Shoes*!	This book offers a great number of problem-solving scenarios. Setting up a pet shop would provide a useful starting point but some children would simply enjoy working out what they could buy for different amounts of money.

suggests that the biggest difference in problem solving between high- and low-achieving pupils lies in the way they record (or represent) what they are doing. She gives the example of students finding out how many squares there are on a chess board. All recognised the nature of the problem but those that failed, failed because they were not systematic. Practice in representing ideas clearly and accessibly will be time well spent.

- *Discussion and collaboration*: these are particularly effective aspects of representation. Resnick (1988) suggests that conflicting views represented in discussion leads the learner to modify or construct their views or ideas. In addition, other minds model different approaches. This is in line with the seminal views of Vygotsky (1978) in which thinking is aligned to conversation. Studies of young children go further, suggesting that thinking and communication are one and the same thing (Goldschmied and Selleck 1996). This aspect of mathematics and problem solving will be explored further in the next chapter.

Worthington and Carruthers (2006) describe some interesting problem-solving activities in which representation and discussion can be seen to have had an important influence. One involves a class of 7- and 8-year-olds going on a picnic. They need nectarines, which are sold in packs of three, for 26 children. One child writes a sum $3 \times 9 = 27$ and recognised that one would be left over. A second child simply counted in threes: 3, 6, 9, 12 etc., while a third listed the same numbers writing alongside each multiple of three the number of packs:

3 1
6 2
9 3
12 4 etc.

One initially wrote 3×26 but then switched to using an empty number line, with more success. Another child drew nine sets of three children with one child crossed out in the final set – a box was added with the figure 1 written in it.

A group of younger children, who had been out on a train, worked from one child's statement – 'I bet there's a million seats in the train!' Although only 4 to 6 years of age, the children had lots of ideas about how they could find out. At a child's suggestion, Aaron, from whom the initial idea had come, telephoned the station staff and discovered that each carriage had 75 seats and that there had been 7 carriages. What is particularly interesting about Worthington and Carruthers' commentary is their interest in all the strategies used – every one gives insight into children's thinking. Of course many of the strategies, as one would expect because of the age of the children involved, were incomplete. Several children drew carriages and then attempted to represent large numbers of people or seats within them. Worthington and Carruthers then give a detailed description of a little girl's interesting strategies. After several graphic attempts at finding a solution, she draws 75 squares in a large rectangle and photocopies this so that she has represented the seven carriages. Although they do not come up with a 'right' final answer, the children show immense understanding of the problem. Their engagement stems from their own interest – probably not something the teacher had planned.

These young children demonstrate many of the strategies identified by Polya (cited by Boaler 2009). They worked to understand the problem and they made plans. Some made charts of numbers, some drew their plans. Of particular interest is the planning strategy termed 'trying a smaller case'. Two little girls are described as using ten shells as carriages with two beads in each. Their strategy does not involve the right numbers – since they are dealing with what are for them very big numbers. But it does however explore a useful strategy. Boaler (2009) makes a very important point about this strategy of trying a smaller case. She suggests that low-achieving students find this difficult to do because it clashes with the *ladder of rules* which governs so much teaching of mathematics. Since progress in mathematics is so often seen as being about dealing with bigger and bigger numbers, choosing to deal with small numbers is regarded as failure.

PUZZLES, GAMES AND INVESTIGATIONS

Boaler (2009) attributes her own love of mathematics and that of many other mathematicians to their early experiences – not doing sums and conventional homework but engaging in puzzles and investigations. She quotes from Sarah Flannery's autobiographical book entitled *In Code: A Mathematical Journey* (2002). Flannery was a European young scientist award winner and she writes:

> Strictly speaking it is not true to say that I or my brothers don't get help with maths. We're not forced to take extra classes, or endure gruelling sessions at the kitchen table but almost without our knowing we've been getting help since we were very young – out-of-the-ordinary help of a subtle and playful kind which I think has made us self-confident in problem-solving. Ever since I can remember, my father has given us little problems and puzzles.
>
> (Boaler 2009: 173, citing Flannery)

There are any number of books of mathematical puzzles, one or two of which are suggested below. However, better than giving a child the book to work through is to keep it informal, playful and collaborative. Many games, such as draughts and chess, involve strategic thinking – a reflective session can enable children to explore winning, as well as less successful, strategies. Bearing in mind the importance of learner-initiated problem finding and problem solving, the role of the teacher should always be to get children interested in finding out – remembering that humans have *puzzling minds* (Tizard and Hughes 1986).

Some problems and investigations begin with puzzling out big numbers. *How Big is a Million?* (Milbourne and Riglietti 2007) is a good story, aimed at young children but the poster it contains showing a million stars holds a great sense of wonder even for adults. Some great investigations could begin with that poster. *How Much is a Million?* (Schwartz 1985) is not a story but a fascinating collection of possible facts about millions, billions and trillions. It might be wise to explore this book with the help of Marcus du Sautoy's guide to big numbers (du Sautoy 2009). *Starting from Big Numbers* (Croydon Beam Group 2004) is quite simply a mathematics book but does have lots of ideas for developing children's interest in big numbers.

Quests are the archetypal problem-solving activity. Ronan (2007) describes the quest undertaken by real mathematicians to discover and classify all the building blocks of symmetry. His account, which he describes as a story involving monsters and moonshine, lies beyond the scope of this book but what it does portray is the excitement and suspense which mathematicians take from finding and solving problems. It should be the aim of teaching mathematics creatively to create this sense of excitement in the children we teach.

STARTING WITH THE CHILD?

Eleanor Duckworth (1996) suggests that intellectual development rests on 'having wonderful ideas'. Fisher (2005) has suggested that in order to have wonderful ideas, you must first have many ideas. Duckworth argues that understanding comes about, not by being told, but by having ideas challenged – through talk and action (2001). This means that puzzles and teacher-led investigations will be most effective if children see them as a starting point for their own wonderful ideas. Boaler (2009: 172–3) concludes that:

> All children start their lives motivated to come up with their own ideas . . . and one of the most important things a parent [authors' note: or teacher] can do is to nurture this motivation. This may take extra work in a subject like mathematics, in which children are wrongly led to believe that all of the ideas have been 'had' and their job is simply to receive them, but this makes the task even more important.

FURTHER READING

Andrews, A. and Trafton, P. (2002) *Little Kids – Powerful Problem Solvers*. Portsmouth, NH: Heinemann.

Duckworth, E. (1996) *'The Having of Wonderful Ideas' and Other Essays on Teaching and Learning*. New York: Teachers' College Press.

CHILDREN'S BOOKS

Allen, P. (1988) *Who Sank the Boat?* London: Puffin Books.

Allen, P. (1994) *Mr Archimedes' Bath*. London: Picture Puffins.

Brown, P. (1993) *Moon Jump a Cowntdown*. London: Penguin Books Ltd.

Clement, R. (1995) *Counting on Frank*. Boston: Houghton Mifflin.

Gray, K. and Sharratt, N. (2001) *Eat Your Peas*. London: Red Fox Books.

Horacek, P. (2004) *A New House for Mouse*. London: Walker Books.

Inkpen, M. (1998) *The Great Pet Sale*. London: Hodder Children's Books.

Milbourne A. and Riglietti, S. (2007) *How Big is a Million?* London: Usborne Publishing Ltd.

Rempt, F. and Smit, N. (2006) *Snail's Birthday Wish*. London: Boxer Books.

Ross, T. (2002) *Centipede's 100 Shoes*. London: Andersen Press Ltd.

Sayre, A. and Sayre, J. (2006) *One is a Snail Ten is a Crab*. Somerville, MA.: Candlewick Press.
Scamell, R. and Terry, M. (2006) *Ouch!* London: Little Tiger Press.
Schwartz, D. (1985) *How Much is a Million?* New York: Harper Trophy.

PUZZLES AND INVESTIGATIONS

Pappas, T. (1997) *The Adventures of Penrose the Mathematical Cat*. San Carlos, CA: Wide World Publishing.
Scieszka, J. and Smith, L. (1995) *Math Curse*. London: Penguin Books.

CHAPTER 4

DEVELOPING UNDERSTANDING: TALKING AND THINKING ABOUT MATHEMATICS

> The universe cannot be read until we have learnt the language and become familiar with the characters in which it is written. It is written in mathematical language, and the letters are triangle, circles and other geometrical figures without which it is humanly impossible to comprehend a single word
>
> (Galileo (1623) cited by Hilliam 2004: 171)

Mathematicians and educators alike are agreed that mathematics both is and has a language of its own (du Sautoy 2008; Boaler 2009; Mercer and Littleton 2007; Alexander 2010). Marcus du Sautoy (2008: 4) describes going with his father to buy some books recommended by his teacher. He writes:

> When I got home I started looking at the books we'd bought. *The Language of Mathematics* particularly intrigued me . . . I'd never thought of mathematics as a language. At school it seemed to be just numbers that you could multiply or divide, add or subtract, with varying degrees of difficulty. But as I looked through this book I could see why my teacher had told me to 'find out what maths is really about'.

In a chapter entitled 'What's going wrong in classrooms?' Boaler (2009) highlights a number of factors. She suggests that there are two main problems. Tests and targets are part of the problem, and the absence of reality is identified as the other. Both learning without thought and learning without talking are questioned. Learning without thought arises for Boaler when children are simply told what to do without fully understanding why. She quotes a girl seen to be doing very well at school as saying that she can get right answers but since she doesn't understand why particular rules give you a right answer, the process has no meaning or satisfaction. In short, it is not creative. Boaler writes 'it is ironic that maths, a subject that should be all about inquiring, thinking and reasoning is one that students have come to believe requires *no thought*' (2009: 37).

The other major aspect of what Boaler calls *passive maths* is the lack of dialogue, or learning without talking. She highlights the immense difference between listening and talking. The words of Sarah Flannery are quoted:

> The first thing I realized about learning mathematics was that there is a hell of a difference between, on the one hand, *listening* to maths being talked about by someone else and thinking that you are understanding, and, on the other, thinking about maths and understanding it yourself and *talking* about it to someone else.
>
> (Boaler 2009: 41, citing Flannery)

This highlights the other theoretical strand that underpins this chapter, namely the link between thinking and communication. Goldschmied and Selleck (1996), in writing about babies, go so far as to suggest that communication (including non-verbal communication, gesture and facial expression) *is* thinking. Siegel (1999) supports this view by writing about the impact of attachment between adults and babies on cognition. In his view (and that of many subsequent writers) the bond that forms between the child and his or her principal caregiver enables the infant to become aware of another mind at work. The link between talk and thought is further underlined by Vygotsky (1986) who writes of speech as the outward form of thought – which over time gradually becomes internalised. Even as adults, we have an intuitive view that talking things through helps us to understand what we think. It is also true that speaking our thoughts out loud often changes and reshapes them.

MATHEMATICAL THINKING AND TALKING

There is widespread agreement that too much of mathematics lesson time, even in primary schools (Boaler 2009), is spent in silence. Resnick (1988), in proposing an approach to mathematics education which involves an emphasis on the ill-structured aspects of mathematics, on problem solving and on what she terms 'sense-making', activities highlights the role of discussion. For her, it is only through talk that children can come to understand and develop an ability to think about mathematics. She compares the small amount of discussion about mathematics with the significantly greater amount of time that is spent in discussion in English, social studies and even science. This, as we saw in the previous chapter, is because 'Educators typically treat mathematics as a field with no open questions and no arguments, at least none that young students or those not particularly talented in mathematics can appreciate' (Resnick 1988: 4).

This lack of talk about mathematics is linked to a lack of practice or rehearsal of ideas and therefore an absence of relevant vocabulary. This is turn means that children have difficulty in talking about mathematics and, if we agree that talk and thought are inextricably linked, inevitably means that children will have difficulty in thinking about mathematics. Whether you take a Piagetian line that action shapes thinking and that this precedes the related language, or the Vygotskian line that talk shapes thinking and that understanding is linked to both (Keenan 2002), the gap between the mathematics that we ask children to do and the language they have to describe it presents a problem. This is further compounded when we acknowledge that much of the mathematics with which we present children is written. The symbols and signs which are used are in themselves a third language.

The Rose Review (Rose 2009) suggests that mathematical understanding is supported by communication. The report highlights the importance of discussion and of learning mathematical language. Children should have opportunities to reflect on and discuss mathematical investigations in order to strengthen their ability to represent their ideas or thinking and to reason or argue them through with others. Rose also underlines the role that drama can play in enabling children to explore language and ideas.

It was a belief in the potential of dramatic play to support children's learning that inspired MakeBelieve Arts to develop a programme of work entitled *Dramatic Mathematics* (Lee 2003). Aimed at Key Stage 1, this resource (available from MakeBelieve Arts) includes five stories that explore place value, subtraction, standard and non-standard measurement, positional language, and division, bringing the subjects to life through drama. The impetus for this programme came from a combination of Kieran Egan's approach to *Teaching as Storytelling*, (Egan 1988, see chapter 6) and MakeBelieve Arts' own commitment to kinaesthetic learning.

Talking about pattern

Upitis *et al.* (1997) refer to the process of exploring, rehearsing and exchanging mathematical ideas as 'mathematicking'. Pattern, an aspect of mathematics which is given insufficient emphasis in school, is a good subject through which to explore the role of language. Eileen, a class teacher, describes (Upitis *et al.* 1997: 43) how pupils involved in a weaving project learned to talk about pattern through presenting their work to others:

> Pupils had to use estimation, predication, trial and error, and planning strategies just to see if their weaving patterns would work . . . The important thing was that each pupil experienced success, each pupil communicated mathematically to the group, and each pupil used mathematics to make something of personal value.

Pattern offers a good example of the way in which the gap between language and understanding operates. The seminal work of the mathematician Hardy was amongst the first to link pattern to mathematics, yet today it is regularly identified as such. He wrote that 'A mathematician, like a painter or a poet, is a maker of patterns. If his patterns are more permanent than theirs, it is because they are made with ideas' (Hardy 1992: 84).

When young children create a picture which is not representational they will often describe it as a pattern. The most common adult response is to admire the pattern without offering any vocabulary which could help the child to think about pattern. Symmetry is a term which regularly comes up when children are engaging with materials such as pattern blocks or when specific work on symmetry is planned.

However, adults rarely apply it to other aspects of learning or to everyday lives. But patterns do not have to be symmetrical. They may be cyclical, repeating, growing, decreasing and so on.

Even adults have some difficulty in defining pattern but there is general consensus that it involves order, regularity, logic and structure (see for example Devlin 2000; Resnik 1999). However it also involves some subjective thinking. Devlin (2000: 72, citing Sawyer) refers to regularities 'that can be recognised by the mind'. Thus a pattern might be about numbers but it might also be about nature or human behaviour. Look closely at the pattern of a tiger's stripes, for example, and you will see that they are not regular. However, you (or in Devlin's terms, your mind) will have no difficulty in recognising the pattern as belonging to a tiger. These ideas are complex for children to take on but through discussion children can learn to think about difficult concepts. The discussion with others promotes collaborative thinking.

Talking mathematically

Learning to talk mathematically has been likened to learning a foreign language (Worthington and Carruthers 2006). Lee (2006: 2) confirms this analogy:

> for many pupils learning to use language to express mathematical ideas will be similar to learning a foreign language . . . Unless the pupils know about the way that language is used in mathematics they may think that they do not understand

SOME CLASSROOM ACTIVITIES TO ENCOURAGE THE DEVELOPMENT OF MATHEMATICAL LANGUAGE

Children can begin to engage in talking in a mathematical language through simple activities. Place two children back to back and place in one of their hands a white board and pen and in the other a shape or picture or pattern. The child with the picture has to describe to their partner the image they are holding so that their partner can reproduce an accurate representation of it on their white board. The description should include where the object is placed on the page, the length of each line or curve. Children have been observed measuring with their fingers the distance from the top of the page to the start of the image and describing this to their partner. Once the activity is completed let the pupils have time to talk together about what instructions would have helped to make the reproduction more accurate. The more often activities like this are repeated the more accurate the mathematical language used in the description becomes.

Another approach to engaging children in developing the language of mathematical description is to give children in pairs a small object which one of them has to hide whilst their partner is blindfolded. The pupil who has hidden the object then has to describe to their partner the exact location, using directional and positional language, including how many paces forward and so on. This type of activity can be extended by creating masking tape roads on the floor where pupils have to guide their blindfolded partners ensuring they don't walk off the path. The activity can be made more challenging by allowing children to offer only a certain number of instructions to their partner in order to help them reach the other end.

a certain concept when what they cannot do is express the idea in language. Conversely, being able to express their mathematical ideas clearly enables pupils to know that they understand and can use mathematical ideas. Teachers will extend their pupils' ability to learn mathematics by helping them to express their ideas using appropriate language and by recognising that they need to use language in a way that is different from their everyday use.

Devlin (2002: 338) maintains that learning to use the language of mathematics enables us to see worlds beyond imagination. By learning to talk about mathematics, we represent and come to understand it better. He writes that 'mathematics is the science of patterns, in the physical universe, in the living world, or even in our own minds . . . mathematics serves us by making the invisible visible' (Devlin 2002: 338). He gives examples of the ways in which this occurs – in the past, long before the advent of spacecraft or powerful telescopes, mathematicians were able to show that planets, including the earth, were round. Similarly probability studies and statistics enable us to predict, seeing into the future.

TALKING TO THINK CREATIVELY

The English National Curriculum for mathematics and QCDA's suggestions about creativity both highlight the importance of talk for thinking. The National Strategy website (National Strategies 2006: 6) highlights the need to 'engage with children's thinking, giving sufficient time for dialogue and discussion and space to think'. In order to engage with children's thinking, it is necessary to support children in talking enough. Research over many decades (Claxton 2008) has indicated that teachers consistently give children too little time to respond thoughtfully. This is often because discussion is taking place in large groups where pace and control become more important than thinking and learning. If we want children to talk and think mathematically the same creative approach is needed. Pringle (2008: 47, citing Prentice) suggests that experiential learning is vital to creativity and that the skills to be nurtured are 'enquiry, reflection and criticism'. In short, children need exciting experiences to talk about and opportunities to talk about them.

QCDA's website (http://www.qcda.gov.uk/) includes advice on promoting creativity. It suggests that teachers wishing to promote creativity should:

- Actively encourage pupils to question, make connections, envisage what might be and explore ideas. Promote and reward imagination and originality.
- Ask open-ended questions such as 'What if . . .?' and 'How might you . . .?' to help pupils see things from different perspectives.
- Value and praise what pupils do and say. Establish an atmosphere in which they feel safe to say things, take risks and respond creatively.
- Create a fun, relaxed working environment if you want to encourage pupils to be adventurous and explore ideas freely.
- Create conditions for quiet reflection and concentration if you want to encourage pupils to work imaginatively.

Teachers are used to asking questions in order to assess learning – and these are often, almost by definition, closed questions. Open-ended questions have many possible answers and as such do not require children to guess what's in the teacher's head but to think for themselves. Praise needs to be specific – in order to reproduce what they are being praised for they need to know what was good about it. So rather than simply saying 'brilliant' or 'well done', adults need to get into the habit of saying things like 'I really liked the way you solved the problem. You were the only one who had that particular idea.'

THINKING THROUGH TALK

Charles Darwin is reported to have likened mathematicians to 'a blind man in a dark room looking for a black cat which isn't there'. This statement in itself has the potential to trigger thought. Philosophy is a discipline to develop critical, logical and reflective thinking. It encourages analytical questioning enabling us to unpick our thought processes and explore their hidden depths. Piaget suggested that children are not capable of philosophical thought until reaching the age of 11 or 12, but Matthews (1980) believes that Piaget simply failed to identify this kind of thinking in the children he studied. Matthews provides examples of very young children engaged in philosophical questioning. An inquiring five-year-old Jordon asked:

> If I go to bed at eight and get up at seven in the morning, how do I really know that the little hand of the clock has gone around only once? Do I have to stay up all night to watch it? If I look away even for a short time, maybe the small hand will go around twice.
>
> (Matthews 1980: 3)

The relationship between philosophy and mathematics is far from new. Many classical philosophers such as Euclid and Archimedes, Pythagoras and Plato were also mathematicians (Berlinghoff and Gouvea 2004). Their interest grew out of an attempt to understand the roles of these subjects in our lives; to explore the link between mathematics and nature. They were men of sufficient means to spend their time thinking and talking – in short to explore some 'slow ways of knowing' (Claxton 1997). It is perhaps paradoxical that mathematical enquiry, grown out of human attempts throughout history to make sense of the world, has become what is seen by so many to be a dry and irrelevant subject.

Philosophy for Children

Philosophy for Children (P4C) was first developed by Matthew Lipman who as a professor at Columbia University in New York became increasingly aware of the undeveloped reasoning skills of many of his students (Lipman 2003). His determination to develop these skills through the teaching of logic led him to develop a programme of work that would tap into what he believed to be children's natural ability to think in the abstract from an early age. He argued that incorporating logical thinking skills

EVERYDAY MATHEMATICS

In order to counter any notion that mathematics is in any way simply the province of the rich and privileged, we should look at some of the alternative early origins of mathematics. It probably grew out of awareness of our bodies, the world around us and the symmetry that is found in nature. We know that early methods of measuring were based on parts of the body. The Egyptians for example used a cubit, which represents the distance from your elbow to the tip of your middle finger, as a unit of measurement. There is an enthralling, small book on this very subject which children at Key Stage 2 in particular find absolutely fascinating. Entitled *About the Size of It* (Cairns 2007), it examines the way in which humans are drawn to measurements which make human sense to us. Whether we use imperial or metric measurement, the favoured quantities in everyday use relate directly back to human history and bodies.

Obviously the flaws in using non-standard measurement are very apparent, but an understanding that the study of mathematics grew out of human need and continuous dialogue as to how to best respond to the challenges that we faced made its early conception a very real subject. Mathematics was not created to keep children occupied at desks, it was and still is a subject that has the potential to challenge us to think deeply and find understanding in the universe around us (du Sautoy 2008; Ronan 2007).

into primary school children's education would help them to develop their abilities for critical thinking.

Lipman proposed that rather than maintaining an education system that consisted of knowledge being transferred from the teacher to the pupil, a reflective education system should be based around a community of enquiry within the classroom. In Lipman's ideal curriculum, students are stirred to think about the world, and knowledge is revealed to them to be 'ambiguous, equivocal and mysterious' (Lipman 2003: 18). P4C works by presenting children with a stimulus; which could be a reading, an object or perhaps a photograph. The children then take time to formulate philosophical questions that have been stimulated by the source material. This enables pupils to think creatively about their experience of human life. A good philosophical question is one where there isn't a fixed answer, where the solution doesn't immediately come to mind – in short an open-ended question.

The class then begins the process of a community of enquiry; the resulting philosophical dialogue is not a debate. Participants are not trying to persuade others of their point of view but rather to explore as a group the best possible answer to the question. P4C is based on the notion that there is no right or wrong answer. As all the participants share their ideas each individual has the opportunity to reflect on the thoughts of their peers.

P4C has the potential to develop in children their abilities to evaluate reasons and arguments. It helps in enhancing pupils' aptitude to make distinctions between differing viewpoints as well as to see the underlying connections between them. The discipline can support children in formulating questions, clarifying their ideas, testing generalities and analysing concepts. These analytical thinking skills would support children in mathematical problem finding and solving.

As we have examined in earlier chapters, one of the biggest challenges facing mathematics today is that it is too often viewed as a subject with only one answer. Developing a community of enquiry within our classrooms enables us to support children in developing their courage to take risks and try different approaches as part of a process of discovery. The further we move away from the fixed notion of mathematics as right or wrong, the more we can open our pupils eyes to the awe and wonder of the universe that has enabled us to develop mathematical systems that are still being shaped today.

The role and impact of philosophy in primary mathematics

Marie France Daniel (1999: 6) draws attention to the gap between everyday and mathematical thinking and language:

> For instance, if they often talk about truth, they rarely question mathematical truth; if they often ask for proof, they seldom ask for mathematical demonstration; if they often compare the number of stars to the infinite, they rarely talk about infinite numbers . . . This is to say, that mathematical language is formed of particular words whose meanings do not always correspond to those in daily language.

Daniel's suggested approach to introducing philosophical-mathematical dialogue into the classroom is to create a community of enquiry where children are invited to clarify the meanings of mathematical words and concepts that they are using frequently without question. Setting these up as a dialogue for the class to explore together will ensure that each child is supporting each other in exploring these terms and trying to find meaning behind them:

> The fostering of creative mathematical thinking may help children create new useful concepts to better understand a theory; to discover a formerly unnoticed relation between two elements; to construct useful ordering; to organize the parts of a whole in a different fashion, and so on. . .
>
> (Daniel 1999: 6)

In Daniel's research into philosophy and mathematics, primary school pupils were involved in developing questions prompted through the stimulus of a novel designed specifically for the programme. The novel, written in French, is called *Les Aventures mathématiques de Mathilde et David* (Daniel *et al.* 1996) and asks questions such as:

- Can a room be a cube or does it only look like a cube?
- Do teachers know everything about geometry?
- What is a problem?
- Can animals think mathematically?
- Does zero equal nothing?
- What is mathematical truth?

THE IMPACT OF P4C

In the UK, extensive research has been undertaken into the impact of P4C on pupils' performance and is beginning to indicate that regular involvement in philosophical dialogues has a direct impact on raising pupil attainment in mathematics. In Clackmannanshire in Scotland (Trickey 2007), for example, a research project published in 2007 demonstrated the following:

- the whole population of children gained on average 6.5 standard points on a measure of cognitive abilities after sixteen months of weekly enquiry
- pupils increased their level of participation in classroom discussion by half as much again following six months of weekly enquiry
- teachers doubled their use of open-ended questions over a six-month period
- when pupils left primary school they did not have any further enquiry opportunities yet their improved cognitive abilities were sustained two years into secondary school
- pupils and teachers perceived significant gains in communication, confidence, concentration, participation and social behaviour following six months of enquiry.

In London, alongside its focus on a creative approach to the curriculum, Gallions Primary School uses P4C as a whole-school approach. Pupils are said to be 'eager to discuss the merits of P4C and the added value they get from this subject that can be reflected across the whole curriculum'. One pupil is quoted as saying:

> Philosophy's helped me in maths. When we're doing problem-solving, the problems sometimes have three, four or even five stages to them. In philosophy we have to break it down to our understanding bit by bit, and that's what we have to do with our maths word problems.
>
> (http://www.teachingexpertise.com/articles/philosophy-for-children-emotional-literacy-in-year-6–2928, accessed 10 February 2010)

OFSTED noted in its 2009 report on the school that 'The children develop listening skills very well, particularly through philosophy lessons, which encourage them to talk about and develop questions for problem-solving'.

STARTING POINTS FOR P4C DIALOGUES

In order for effective dialogues to take place children need to be presented with a stimulus that will inspire them to ask philosophical mathematical questions. Throughout this book numerous suggestions of stories that provoke mathematical enquiry are made. In the previous chapter, work focused around *Mr Archimedes' Bath* (Allen 1994) was described. Pamela Allen (1988) also wrote *Who Sank the Boat?* This story raises questions around how something as small as a mouse can make such a big difference, a theme also explored in the traditional story of *The Enormous Turnip.*

MATHS FOCUS *PHILOSOPHY AND MATHS*

- *Probability:* What are the chances of winning money in the national lottery?
- *Mental maths and mathematical judgement:* How quickly can you work out which is the best choice from a series of '*Would You Rather*' questions?
- *Reasoning:* Critical thinking around the choices we make under time-pressure
- *Analytical thinking:* Talking about maths and problems rather than worrying about getting the right answer

Scenario

Warm-up exercise: *Would You Rather . . .?*

- Win £100
- Receive 1 pence on one day, 2 pence on the second day, 4 pence on the third day and this continue to double every day for one month
- Win £1,800 that you had to split with 12 people
- Receive what was left from £5,000, where each day for a week it was reduced by 10%.

Dialogue stimulus – a Lottery ticket

Exploration

1. Warm-up exercise – *Would You Rather . . .?*
   Pupils were given the above series of '*Would You Rather*?' questions which they were asked to choose between quickly, without having time to work out the mathematical answer. They were then invited to discuss their choices with the rest of the class.
2. Dialogue stimulus – a Lottery ticket
   The group, who had previous experience of creating philosophical dialogues, were invited to create philosophical questions around the stimulus of a Lottery ticket. They then took part in a dialogue on the probability of gambling.

Outcomes

- The question that was chosen for dialoguing was 'Is the lottery a waste of £1 or are you buying hope?'
- Other questions included 'Does gambling pay?' 'What is hope?' 'Is the lottery a waste of money?' 'Should gambling money be used to help poor people?'
- Pupils used mathematical language to talk about probability and the chances of winning money on the lottery.
- The group of Year 6 pupils became very engrossed in the dialogue which lasted for 45 minutes.

Quotes from evaluation

I have realised through philosophy that I don't always know the answer. But in maths we are always supposed to know the answer. Today I just had more questions: is it alright to waste money if it makes you happy?

Year 6 pupil

continued . . .

MATHS FOCUS ***PHILOSOPHY AND MATHS*** . . . *continued*

Further information

Although MakeBelieve Arts created this dialogue with Year 6 pupils, it is possible to engage much younger children in philosophy and mathematics using some of the starting points exampled below.

I'm Coming To Get You (Ross 2008) may influence a dialogue on size and shape or questions around how big a monster is. The underlying question in this book is, however, questions around fear and relative power. *365 Penguins* (Fromental and Jolivet 2006) is full of mathematical ideas but there are other underlying philosophical questions to do with conservation and responsibility.

COLLABORATION

All of this requires a very different environment than that in which mathematics is so often taught, a topic to which we will return in Chapter 12. In underlining the importance of discussion in mathematics education, Boaler (2009: 44) highlights the relationship between talking and thinking. She writes:

> when we verbalize mathematical thoughts we need to reconstruct them in our minds, and when others react to them we reconstruct them again. This act of reconstruction deepens understanding. When we work on mathematics in solitude there is only one opportunity to understand the mathematics.

Children learn not only from the reconstruction in their own head but from other people's reconstructions and explanations. This is similar to the creative act which involves review and modification (NACCCE 1999) and to the translation from one medium to another which is basis of education in the preschools of Reggio Emilia (Edwards *et al.* 1998). Vygotsky referred to this process as transduction (Kress 1996) and regarded it as an important strand in promoting understanding. In particular, the process of collaboration gives children access to a wider range of problem-solving strategies (Mercer and Littleton 2007).

Being encouraged to discuss more within the primary classroom can have a massive effect on how pupils work together. As one Year 6 pupil says:

> It's changed a lot – we used to have to sit down and just do it, now we can work with each other. It's more exciting and if you get stuck you can ask the other person and they can help you. It's like if you get stuck you know you have someone to catch you when you fall.

This view is echoed by Lee (2006) who suggests that characteristics of a discourse community, or collaborative group, are trust and respect for others (having someone to catch you when you fall); a sense of contributing (we work with each other) and an awareness of the identity of others (you can ask and they can help).

THE WRITTEN LANGUAGE OF MATHEMATICS

We don't want to leave this chapter without reference to the written language of mathematics. Worthington and Carruthers (2006) argue that children have to become bi-literate in order to become successful mathematical thinkers. This requires, they believe, opportunities in the early years to develop an understanding of the ways in which graphical representations including drawings and numerals promote understanding. The National Strategy in England also highlights the important role of representation in thinking mathematically, advising teachers to 'demonstrate the correct use of mathematical vocabulary, language and symbols, images, diagrams and models as tools to support and extend thinking' (National Strategies 2006: 6). 'Demonstrate' is perhaps a poor choice of words in this context since it could indicate the passive experience for children which Boaler (2009) insists we should be moving away from. Representation is something that learners must engage in fully if they are to understand it – not something they can simply be told about and shown.

In the next chapter, there will be some discussion about the use of manipulatives and structured apparatus. These may act (and were devised) as a form of representation but different representations work differently for different learners. This means that children need to be able to choose from a wide range of resources, and teachers need to be willing to tune into the way in which children are thinking things through. This is true whether the answer which children arrive at is right or wrong. Having to describe a successful strategy is as useful as having to explain an unsuccessful one. Both give the teacher insight into children's thinking and both give the learner insight into his or her own thinking.

FURTHER READING

Lee, C. (2006) *Language for Learning Mathematics*. Maidenhead: Open University Press.

Mercer, N. and Littleton, K. (2007) *Dialogue and the Development of Children's Thinking*. London: Routledge.

CHILDREN'S BOOKS

Allen, P. (1988) *Who sank the Boat?* London: Penguin Books.

Fromental, J-L. and Jolivet, J. (2006) *365 Penguins*. New York: Abrams Books for Young Children.

Reynolds, P. (2007) *So Few of Me*. London: Walker Books.

This book explores the language of few, less and so on. It will strike a chord with every teacher. Leo the hero has so much to do. He dreams of nine other Leos coming to help him but the list of things to do just grows longer, until he realises that 'just me, just one . . . with time to dream' is enough.

Ross, T. (2008) *I'm Coming To Get You*. London: Andersen Press.

CHAPTER 5

TEACHING MATHEMATICS CREATIVELY: REAL MATHS!

Everyday things hold wonderful secrets for those who know how to observe and tell about them.

(Rodari, cited by Castagnetti and Vecchi 1997: 12)

REAL BECAUSE IT IS CONNECTED TO OUR OWN EXPERIENCE OF MATHEMATICS?

For many children and adults, mathematics is real when it conforms to established expectations about what maths is. In school it is often interpreted as learning to do everyday calculations which could be applied to real life – the problem so often is that children fail to make the connections which can seem very obvious to the adults involved. Drummond (2003) gives an example of a child in Year 3 working through a test sheet. Many of the test items were rooted in everyday experiences – comparing heights and money transactions for example. And yet, whether abstract sums or everyday problems, the child's response is an apparently meaningless string of numbers. Drummond suggests that the teachers' approaches have conflicted with his right to learn. She continues:

> We can also see how Jason has accepted his responsibilities as a pupil, including his responsibility to comply with his teachers, who have treated his compliance as a pupil as if it alone were a sufficient and satisfactory outcome of their teaching. They seem to have lost sight of their responsibility to use their power in the interests of learning, rather than simply as an instrument of social control. Jason's quest for meaning emphasises his teachers' responsibility constantly to check whether the world they invite Jason to inhabit as a pupil is one that makes sense to him as a child.
>
> (Drummond 2003: 10)

But teachers are not heartless or thoughtless: they act in this way because they feel pressure from above – headteachers, parents, inspectors and even media. In addition, however, perhaps the reasons why so many adults focus on abstract calculations through sums (whether written or oral) and worksheets is because they themselves lack confidence. It takes confidence (and expertise) to explain to parents the mathematical learning that occurred in a drama session; or to explain why playing in the shop is about more than getting the shopping sums right. It takes confidence (and reflection) to explore what the differences might be between real and fake mathematics (Boaler 2009).

Perhaps above all it takes confidence to deal with questions from children to which you do not have a ready answer. Mathematics based on a worksheet or a section of a textbook has its own answer sheet – a maths session based around composing a song or working through a problem identified by a group of children has no prescribed answers and may involve many unexpected questions. For the high proportion of people who lack confidence in their own mathematical ability – which inevitably will statistically include some teachers and support staff – this can be quite scary. However, the more adults recognise the importance of exploring mathematics which does not always have right answers and easy solutions, the more able they will be to accept the challenge.

MAKING IT REAL THROUGH THE USE OF STRUCTURED MATERIALS

Many attempts to bridge the gap between concrete (or real world) mathematics and the abstract have focused on developing and using structured apparatus. It has been suggested that what American writers term mathematical 'manipulatives', that is 'physical objects specifically designed to foster learning' of mathematics (Zuckerman *et al.* 2005), stem from two main sources. The first source is Froebel's Gifts which were developed during the first half of the nineteenth century. The Gifts include a set of structured wooden shapes, beginning with a cube, cylinder and sphere and working up to a collection of complex cubes, cuboids, triangles and prisms which together made up an 8 inch cube (Pound 2005; Read 1992) and are said to have led to the development of familiar structured materials such as wooden blocks, K'nex and Lego. Zuckerman *et al.* (2005: 859) describe these as 'design materials, fostering modeling on real-world structures'.

The second source they identify is the work of another pioneer of early childhood education, Maria Montessori, in the first half of the twentieth century. Her approach to mathematics education was to use carefully structured and beautifully made materials. Bead frames (or abacuses) and wooden hierarchical materials still form the basis of mathematics teaching and can be found on Montessori websites (e.g. http://www.infomontessori.com). Zuckerman *et al.* (2005) suggest that these materials have led to the development of materials such as Cuisenaire rods and Colour Factor – both of which were very popular in the 1960s. The more recent development of materials such as Numicon is also part of this legacy, which is described as fostering the 'modeling of more abstract structures'.

The use and role of structured materials in teaching and learning mathematics is not without debate. A study by Moyer (2001) considered teachers' use of structured materials in the middle years of schooling. She found that many teachers regarded them as little more than fun, or a diversion from more traditional modes of teaching. She also found that where teachers did not have a strong grasp of the concepts they were attempting to teach, the use of materials made little difference to children's understanding and learning.

Some studies seem to indicate that computer images (Booth and Siegler 2008; Clements 2000; Uttal *et al.* 1997) or 'virtual manipulatives' do have some positive impact on learning. Moyer *et al.* differentiate these from static visual representations in that they are dynamic and allow children to 'slide, flip and turn . . . [the representation] as if it were a three-dimensional object' (2002: 37). The authors (Moyer *et al.* 2002: 377) conclude that the uses of virtual manipulatives 'are limited only by the creativity of the teachers and students who work with them'.

Clements (2000) raises an interesting debate about what is meant by concrete experience. He regards it not as an opposite to abstract but sees both concrete and abstract as part of a cluster of ways of thinking about difficult concepts. He echoes the views of Moyer (2001) and Moyer *et al.* (2002) that teachers' skills and knowledge base determine the effectiveness of structured materials, citing research which suggests that 'Attitudes towards mathematics are improved when students have instruction with concrete materials provided by teachers knowledgeable about their use' (Clements 2000: 46, citing Sowell).

Achievements and attitudes are not improved where the materials are not used in a way which supports exploration; or where children do not make links between the two symbol systems involved – structured materials and numerals. This is linked to a third barrier between linking concrete and abstract thought – which is that for manipulatives to be used successfully, teachers need to review the way in which ideas are represented more generally. This is where creative arts can be seen to be of great importance – an aspect of teaching and learning which will be explored more fully in Chapter 8.

Clements (2000: 49) differentiates between sensory-concrete and integrated-concrete ideas. He writes:

> *Sensory-concrete* refers to knowledge that demands the support of concrete objects and children's knowledge of manipulating these objects. *Integrated-concrete* refers to concepts that are 'concrete' at a higher level because they are connected to other knowledge, both physical knowledge that has been abstracted and thus distanced from concrete objects and abstract knowledge of a variety of types.

He argues, citing the Piagetian theorist Kamii, not simply that children must be physically active but that 'good concrete activity is good *mental* activity' (Clements 2000: 50). He further suggests that the use of virtual manipulatives can work hand in hand with concrete sensory and integrated experiences. He believes that this provides benefits for both teachers and learners. One difficulty is often that teachers fail to make, and children fail to see, the connections between the apparatus (virtual or otherwise) and the purpose of the abstract ideas which the materials are supposed to be representing. On the other hand, some children become engrossed in the patterns and come to enjoy the beauty of the mathematics revealed by the structured apparatus itself.

REAL BECAUSE IT REFLECTS EVERYDAY LIFE?

Sometimes when reference is made to real maths, the focus is on functional mathematics – the kind of mathematics which we use in our everyday lives. This is generally seen as being about everyday events such as shopping; sharing out biscuits; working out mileage and so on. Creative teachers will see the mathematical potential in creating real experiences such as cooking, a camping trip or end-of-term party. Events and activities such as these offer plenty of mathematical learning opportunities.

The case study below is based on *The Doorbell Rang* (Hutchins 1989). Sharing cookies, the topic of the book, is a familiar and real experience. Gifford (2005) describes a piece of research in which young children's approach to problem solving was explored. Children were asked to share out fairly varying numbers of biscuits to different numbers of children. After several variations, one enterprising child simply crumbled all the biscuits and doled out roughly equal amounts of crumbs. To their credit, the researchers recorded this as a good problem-solving strategy.

Andrews and Trafton (2002) describe work based on this book. Unlike the children in Hutchins' book, these children were given different biscuits. Sharing these highlights children's keen sense of fairness. The authors describe the children's strategies and write:

> The children assigned a value of 2 to the chocolate cookies and a value of 1 to the vanilla cookies . . . What made the two groups of cookies 'equal' in the

MATHS FOCUS ***THE DOORBELL RANG***

- *Estimation:* How many biscuits do you estimate there are in a packet?
- *Problem solving:* How should we share out the biscuits?
- *Pattern:* How many biscuits fit on different size trays without overlapping? What patterns can we make with our biscuits? *The Doorbell Rang* contains short repetitive phrases that set out the pattern of the story. Involve children in looking at patterns of stories and creating stories with the pattern of a recurring phrase.
- *Computation:* How many biscuits do we need for different numbers of children?
- *Data gathering:* What data can you gather on the unknown number of cookies grandma brings at the end and the number of children yet to arrive? Involve children in estimating how many cookies might be on grandma's plate and how many children it would feed.

Scenario

Two children attempt to share out 12 cookies equally between them. The cookies have been made by their mother and the children think that they look and smell as good, 'but no-one makes cookies like grandma'. Just as the children divide the biscuits between them the doorbell rings and two more children arrive. The children begin to share out the biscuits four ways. Again the doorbell rings and now the biscuits need to be shared six ways. As more and more children arrive the shares in the biscuits get smaller till each child is entitled to one

continued . . .

MATHS FOCUS ***THE DOORBELL RANG*** . . . *continued*

each. Then the doorbell rings yet again. Luckily this time it is Grandma and she has bought some more cookies.

Exploration

1 Before reading the book, children were asked how they could share a packet of biscuits with the whole class. They were also asked whether they could estimate from the look of a packet whether each child would be able to have one biscuit each, or if there would be insufficient.
2 Next we explored how we could share just 3 biscuits with the whole class and finally how we could share only 1 biscuit.
3 When we read the story we involved children in physically acting it out, sharing their feelings about the dwindling share of biscuits. We gave each child 12 biscuits and increasing numbers of paper plates so that as we read through the story they could physically create the correct number of piles of biscuits on each plate to correspond with the number of children arriving in the house. We made our biscuits from cut out circles of cardboard which we placed in a biscuit tin.
4 We then gave a group of pupils a preset amount of biscuits for them to divide equally between them. This was repeated so that we used the same number of biscuits but changed the number of pupils.

Outcomes

- As we read the story in one school and the doorbell rang for the fifth time a little boy shouted out, 'hide, and don't open the door'.

Quotes from evaluations

> One biscuit between all of us, we'd have to take just a tiny bit each.
>
> Year 1 pupil

> We'd all have to hold our mouths small like this [purses her lips].
>
> Year 1 pupil

Further information

If you act out the story with children, you may wish to read the book twice so that everyone has an opportunity to be part of dividing the biscuits.

Having tangible materials is important in maths. These don't need to be expensive and can be fun and made from cardboard or objects that you have around you.

Lumps of play-dough can be made into one large biscuit by the children; as the second child arrives the biscuit is cut into half and then into quarters. Children are then invited to explore how to divide the biscuit equally in various ways to make sure all the new guests have a fair share.

References

Hutchins, P. (1989) *The Doorbell Rang*. London: Harper Trophy.

> children's minds was not the number of cookies but the value of them . . . We are forced to rethink what is appropriate mathematics for young children. Mathematical ideas are often withheld from children because the work goes beyond the expectations of what young children should investigate.
>
> (Andrews and Trafton 2002: 25)

The mathematics that is real in many children's lives is often a useful starting point. This may be conscious mathematical knowledge, such as comes from working knowledge of racing pigeons, an understanding of complex card games, scoring darts or the child whose mother runs a slimming club (Gifford 2005). But there is also practical and perhaps unconscious mathematical knowledge which comes from helping adults to construct buildings or engage in DIY; or from playing snooker. All of these are real and can be used to extend mathematical thinking and learning.

Everyday mathematics can also be about allowing children to explore and make sense of the numbers, patterns, shapes and measures they see in the world around them. Mathematics is everywhere, from fantasy football leagues, to working out how long it will take you to get home from the park. So many things we do in our everyday lives have a strong mathematical connection but this is often overlooked within the mathematics curriculum. Yet these offer many creative starting points.

REAL MATHEMATICIANS

The apparent focus on real, everyday mathematics can lead to a situation where teachers highlight what Boaler (2009) calls 'fake maths' while feeling as though they are highlighting 'real maths'. Remember those problems you were presented with at secondary school about swimming pools and men digging holes – it is highly unlikely that the way in which you were taught to set about solving those problems has much in common with what real mathematicians do.

Academic mathematicians have a different view of what constitutes real mathematics. In Chapter 1 we outlined what, for mathematicians, counts as mathematics. For the real mathematician, revelling in challenges or puzzles seems to be of prime importance (du Sautoy 2008; Ronan 2007). In fact, as discussed in Chapter 3, problem finding is at least as important as problem solving, since it arises primarily from interest. Perhaps what is an apocryphal story about Richard Feynes, a Nobel Prize winning physicist, suggests that he found the problem he subsequently worked on and which led to his award, while spinning paper plates in the cafeteria. As discussed in Chapter 1, the solution is often a guess, estimate or approximation. This in turn gives the mathematician a working hypothesis – proving or disproving the hypothesis is likely to involve the hard work stereotypically associated with real mathematicians. At this point, logic, reasoning, measurement and comparison are involved but so are symbolic representation, visualisation and generalisations.

Mathematics is the science of pattern (see Chapter 1). Both Ronan (2007) and du Sautoy (2008) describe the sensitivity to patterns which mathematicians have. Humans, including mathematicians, are often described as pattern-seekers (see for example Lucas 2001). The six-year-old playing with pattern blocks who:

- notices that a hexagon can be made in a number of different ways
- can cope with changing the way in which some of her hexagons are made, and thus
- accommodates a troublesome lack of tiles of the right shape is behaving mathematically – seeing a pattern and generalising it.

Our brains look for patterns and try to identify patterns even where none is readily apparent. It is this which has driven the mathematical search for prime numbers; triangular and perfect numbers and so on – but it is also this which motivates us to do sudokus, kakuros and so on. Pattern-seeking requires a vocabulary to support mathematical thinking and it requires an ability to analyse and generalise from data. National strategy documents (see for example DfES 2006b) describe these qualities as key skills in mathematics for children – but they are also essentially what real mathematicians have to do.

Perhaps more surprising to the lay person is the apparent importance of estimation, guesswork or intuition. Closely linked to this is the need for an ability to represent ideas symbolically and to imagine, visualise and generalise abstract ideas. Devlin (2000) suggests that mathematics is the most abstract subject and that abstract thinking requires imagination. Imagination is a key aspect of creativity – and a number of writers underline the creative nature of mathematics (see for example Mazur 2003; du Sautoy 2008). Again, national strategy documents (DfES 2006b) highlight the creative nature of mathematics and suggest that conjectural questions such as 'what if?' lead to important ideas and mathematical thinking – 'questioning assumptions and conclusions'.

Real mathematicians have in the past often regarded pure mathematics as the only real mathematics. Indeed, Hardy's seminal work (1992, first published 1941), stated the primacy of mathematics which was not applied to everyday life and expressed the view that pure mathematics was not simply, but *ought* to be, useless. This has changed as more and more uses of apparently useless challenges have been found. The sixteenth-century Italian mathematician Cardano developed the idea of cubic equations which in the nineteenth century supported the use of alternating electrical current and in turn the invention of the electric chair. Einstein used geometry developed by ancient Greek philosophers as the basis of his work on relativity which has subsequently been applied in work on global navigation and space travel.

REAL FOR CHILDREN

Perhaps somewhat paradoxically, it is the abstract nature of mathematics which has led teachers of mathematics to search out approaches and strategies which emphasise real and concrete experiences. The thinking has been that, since mathematics is so abstract, children need everyday experiences on which to base their ideas. And this is clearly true. Hughes (1986: 47–8), for example, gives an account of a conversation with four-year-old Patrick. He asks Patrick 'how many is two and one more?'. Patrick answers that it is four. Asked in turn, how many lollipops, elephants or giraffes would two and one more make, he correctly replies three in each case. Hughes returns to the abstract sum – to which Patrick gives the answer six.

Nunes *et al.*'s (1993) account of their work with Brazilian street children demonstrate the ways in which mathematics with a real or embedded (Donaldson 1976) context make human sense to children. It is this knowledge which has led teachers to develop the kind of work based on real experiences like those described above – shopping trips, planning playgrounds or events and so on.

However this is does not seem to be enough. As discussed in Chapter 2, what is real for children does not always conform to what is real for adults. For the five-and six-year-olds described in Italy and in the United States of America, rulers were insufficiently real to be trusted.

Paley (1981), a highly creative teacher, returns from vacation to find a large bag of sand in the classroom. She asks the children to think about how they could move it. Their discussion focuses on some magical solutions, including the magical appearance of Superman. Paley grows excited as the children's on-going discussion leads them to visualise something rather like a pulley. With the help of the science teacher and a pulley, they successfully move the sand. A week later, Paley sets the children a problem – how could they move her without touching her? One child's instant response is 'why?' – a question to which Paley is not unsympathetic. Nonetheless, she persists and is surprised that the children rehearse a similar sequence of thinking to that which had emerged before they had been introduced to the pulley. This time a lever seems to offer a solution. She takes them to a local science museum where levers, pulleys, wheels and ramps are demonstrated. Returning to school, Paley tells a story about a caveman moving a rock. This time the children's solutions again do not include machines but:

- digging a hole under the rock
- getting people and dinosaurs to push
- breaking the rock with a hammer
- finding another cave.

Paley concludes:

> The adult should not underestimate the young child's tendency to revert to earlier thinking; new concepts have not been 'learned' but are only in temporary custody. They are glimpsed and tried out but are not permanent possessions.
>
> (Paley 1981: 101)

Sums are rarely real!

Eight-year-old Jeremy is being told that John has eight bricks and that Mary has three times as many. Silence ensues – eventually the teacher asks him what three times eight is. He at first replies 23 but then corrects that to 24. He is asked a similar question about Andrew having four times as many bricks – with similar results. Questioning reveals that Jeremy believed he should add the numbers given and that he therefore had no idea why the teacher was satisfied with the answer arrived at by multiplication (Hughes 1986, citing Shuard).

The main thrust of Hughes' work is that 'children's observed difficulties can be described as a failure to link the understandings they already have with the symbols and rules they are expected to learn' (1986: 175, citing Hiebert). He continues:

> We have on our side, however, a strength which is often underestimated: the immense capacity of young children to grasp difficult ideas if they are presented in ways which interest them and make sense to them.
>
> (Hughes 1986: 184)

Making it real through drama and role play

Drama and role play make things very real for children. They enable children to explore the feelings and emotions which underpin learning, including the mathematical learning iself. They support children in exploring difficult concepts in non-threatening surroundings. They make it possible for children to weave stories around the understandings they are developing and they give vital opportunities for the discussion and collaboration which shape learning.

Teachers often associate such opportunities with young children. In *Let's Pretend Maths* (Williams 2006), for example, the author makes a number of suggestions about dramatic play opportunities. Although the book is focused on the early years it is easy to see that a shoe shop, a drama centred around pirates, a vet's surgery or a baby clinic, or a travel agency present a wealth of mathematical learning opportunities for older as well as younger children. The case study presented here demonstrates the real impact that such opportunities can have for real, rather than fake, mathematical learning – in this case with a Year 6 class.

Making it real through the use of the imagination

In considering what makes things real for humans we ought not to overlook the power of the imagination. Symbolising ideas and concepts through story, drama, mark-making, music or construction aids thinking. But it is imagination which enables us to visualise – a vital aspect of mathematical abstract thinking. Clements (2004: 42–3) suggests that all children, beginning before kindergarten, should be encouraged to:

> create a mental image of geometric objects, 'examine' it mentally to answer questions about it, and transform it . . . slide, turn and flip shapes mentally . . . All children should work on developing their ability to create, maintain, and represent mental images of geometric shapes and of the environments in which they live.

The widespread use of empty number lines in primary schools (Angliheri 2001) is also a recognition of the role of imagination in learning to think in the abstract.

MATHS FOCUS ***RUBBISH MATHS***

- *Percentages and fractions:* all the offers to take rubbish away are made in a mixture of percentages or fractions.
- *Problem solving:* working together as a team to solve problems.
- *Dealing with money:* keeping a check on the money they are spending and the money they are earning. Working out the best deals.

Scenario

In role as council officers, the workshop leaders stand before the class and pour several bags of rubbish all over the carpet area. The class are told that the local authority has run out of space for the rubbish so any empty areas are being used for storage; their carpet has been selected as a dump. The children begin to complain and are offered money for their inconvenience. The council officer gives each of the four groups £100 and then leaves. The children are invited to sort the rubbish into types so that they can think about what can be done with it. The group collecting plastic has more than those collecting glass. Similarly there is more cardboard than tins. The workshop leader then goes into role as a police officer and the class is fined £100 for not getting rid of the rubbish. They have to work out how to pay this fairly. Should the group with the most rubbish pay the most?

Exploration

1. Children are given cards which tell them about various people who are willing to buy rubbish, or to take some of it away. They have to work out who will give them the best deal. Should they go with an artist who pays good money for specific pieces of rubbish but only wants a few items or to a dealer who won't pay much but will get rid of it? Or should they give 20% of their rubbish to the local nursery and receive no money at all?
2. Their decisions about who to go with are made quickly under the threat that the police will return and fine them for whatever rubbish they have remaining.
3. At the end of an hour of selling, giving away and fining, we find out which group has the most money left.

Outcomes

- Pupils engaged strongly in the activity, the sense of both competition and team work between them was immense.

Quotes from evaluation

> At first I thought having lots of plastics was brilliant. We had so much more rubbish on our table than anyone else. Then the police came and fined us and suddenly we had the least amount of money.
>
> Year 6 child

Further information

When setting up *teacher in role* work it is important to remember you are not trying to make the pupils believe you are the character. If you do adopt this approach you may find they will

continued . . .

MATHS FOCUS ***RUBBISH MATHS*** . . . *continued*

continually try to prove that you are not. We always have a small piece of costume for any 'in role character': a hat, scarf, orange safety bib etc. We show the costume to the pupils and announce, 'When I put this hat on I will no longer be your teacher, but I will become the character of a police officer.'

References

Rubbish Maths is a programme developed and delivered by MakeBelieve Arts (http://www.makebelievearts.co.uk).

Visualising things that are not present to the senses is part of this process (Devlin 2000). However, as with the use of structured apparatus, it appears that this approach is only as good as the teacher using it. Heuvel-Panhuizen (2008) argues that unless the empty number line is used flexibly as a tool for children it can undermine their mathematical thinking. He concludes that teachers should listen more to children and take their views more seriously – recognising their competence and diagnosing their misconceptions more accurately.

We cannot leave the topic of making things real through the use of the imagination without mentioning Einstein. He famously developed 'thought experiments' to develop his thinking, from his adolescence. Isaacson (2007: 3) describes his work thus: 'Imagine being in an enclosed elevator accelerating up through space, he conjectured in one of them. The effects you'd feel would be indistinguishable from the experience of gravity.'

Einstein's use of his imagination included creating pictures in his mind but more unusually:

> such things as lightening strikes and moving trains, accelerating elevators and falling painters, two dimensional blind beetles crawling on curved branches as well as a variety of contraptions designed to pinpoint at least in theory the location and velocity of speeding electrons.
>
> (Isaacson 2007: 27)

CONCLUSION

Making mathematics real involves much more than just focusing on the mathematics we use in our everyday lives. It involves encouraging the use of the imagination and of a host of opportunities for symbolic representation – everything from music and dance, through mark-making and modeling and including the empty number line. Of course, not every child you teach will prove to be an Einstein but given the right creative environment some might become those makers of new mathematical meanings which will be increasingly needed in our society.

FURTHER READING

Moyer, P., Bolyard, J. and Spikell, M. (2002) 'What are virtual manipulatives?', *Teaching Children Mathematics*, 8(6): 372–7.

Williams, H. (2006) *Let's Pretend Maths*. London: BEAM Publications.

CHILDREN'S BOOKS

Crowther, R. (2002) *Shapes*. London: Walker Books.

Although this is a very simple book with flaps and tabs, it is one of the few books that highlights the notion of shape as a construct, rather than a fixed characteristic. Crowther identifies, for example, a bunch of grapes and a hairbrush as having an oval shape – food for thought and discussion.

Hutchins, P. (1989) *The Doorbell Rang*. London: Harper Trophy.

CHAPTER 6

TEACHING MATHEMATICS CREATIVELY: USING STORY TO TEACH MATHS

> The teaching and learning of mathematics in today's schools will change dramatically if we view mathematics as a tool for telling stories. Learners will see mathematics as a consequence of social interaction; they will recognise it as a tool for telling and remembering, not reciting and memorising.
>
> (Whitin and Wilde 1995, xii)

What better way than to begin this chapter than with a story?

> Doris used to follow her mathematics textbook. She would present her fourth graders the lesson in their textbook, give them practice problems, and then assign homework. Homework was checked at the beginning of every math lesson, and a test was given at the end of each week.
>
> About 1990, after teaching this way for 10 years, Doris decided to reinvent the way she taught in order to make teaching more enriching for both her students and herself. First, Doris started using manipulatives. She used base ten blocks, geoboards, pattern blocks, and fraction bars to help give meaning to her lessons. Later she discovered math games: social games with names like addition war, division bingo, and multiplication dominoes. Doris created twenty to thirty math games that reinforced and extended the ideas presented in each chapter of her textbook using materials such as egg cartons, poster board, tongue depressors, and wood cubes.
>
> By 1992 Doris discovered children's literature and began using mathematical stories with her class. She felt, however, that few children's storybooks developed the mathematical skills that she wanted her children to learn and that when she read a book to her students they were outsiders looking in on the world of others. She wanted to get her class more fully involved in mathematical stories

> – involved in ways that deeply stimulated their fantasies and more fully developed the mathematical skills that she wanted them to learn.
>
> (Schiro 2004: 3)

This story, like many others, resonates with the experiences of many of us. In attempting to make mathematics more real and accessible, many different approaches have been developed. In England, the National Curriculum and NNS have shaped many helpful changes and responses but the message remains similar – mathematics education is not working in its current form. Creative approaches are needed.

MAKEBELIEVE ARTS' STORY

This story takes a different path than that explored by Doris. Spurred on by the work of Egan (1988) MakeBelieve Arts began by creating strong stories to be told and performed in classrooms. Over time, as we attempted to introduce these ideas to teachers in CPD sessions three things became apparent:

1. Full involvement in mathematical stories should mean that teachers could develop their own stories to tie into children's current interests and enthusiasms.
2. Most teachers, like Doris, found it difficult to spare the time or felt that they lacked the aptitude to develop stories of their own.
3. Most primary teachers, perhaps unlike Doris, have a wealth of knowledge about children's books. It may also be that more suitable books are more available in this country or at this time.

WHY STORY IS IMPORTANT

Through centuries of exposure to story form, our brains have become hardwired to respond to stories. If someone begins to recite a story, they have the power to make a room fall silent; people can't help but be drawn in. As we hear the first few sentences the neurons in our brain begin to fire, we begin to anticipate what might happen, we make assumptions as to what will come next, and we sift through our knowledge of this type of story and begin to build up expectations of the likely outcome. When we listen to stories we focus on key characters and fill in the gaps about them based on our own experiences and knowledge. We understand their motivations and drives without needing lengthy descriptions of these. The way the brain works to decipher story is highly sophisticated and yet there is much evidence to prove that we are able to engage in this process from a very young age.

Paley (1997) labels story making as an original learning tool that humans have used throughout history and that children continue to use in order to understand and make sense of the world. Children at play will try things out, refine them, come back to them, look at them from another angle, bring in other children to support the idea they are exploring, change roles and find reasons and solutions to problems that seem insurmountable. These are the same kinds of engagement that we want our children to have in relation to mathematical enquiry and understanding.

Paley suggests that current marginalisation of play and narrative in the teaching and learning process is akin to discovering a way to integrate all the teachings that were required to become a doctor, but deciding to revert to the old ways of teaching:

> Is this not, in effect, what happens to our children when they enter school? For five years, an intuitive program called play has worked so well that the children learn the language, mannerisms, and meaning of all the people with whom they live. They know what every look means, every tone of voice, who their family is, where they come from, what makes them happy or sad, what place they occupy in the world. Then the children enter school and find, strangely enough, that this natural theater they have been performing, this playfully deep fantasy approach to life is no longer acceptable, is no longer valid. Suddenly they begin to hear . . . 'Do that playing outside, after your work'.
>
> (Paley 1997)

Research and writings from a wide variety of disciplines show that as humans we have not only a predisposition but a need for story (see for example Haven 2007; Paley 1990; Bruner 1986; Pinker 2000; Devlin 2000). Haven (2007) explores the vital role that story plays in our lives and the potential it has to engage us in learning. He cites both Bruner and Pinker in his argument for the true power behind story:

> Humans have an inherent readiness or predisposition to organize experience into story form: into viewpoints, characters, intentions, sequential plot structures, and the rest.
>
> (Haven nd: 20, citing Bruner)

> 100,000 years of evolutionary preference for, and reliance on, STORY has built into the human genetic code instructions to wire the brain to think in story terms by birth.
>
> (Haven nd: 20, citing Pinker)

Haven (2007: 27) identities three key truths that have emerged from recent neurological research:

1. One hundred thousand years of human reliance on story has evolutionarily rewired the human brain to be predisposed to think in story terms and to use story structure to create meaning and make sense of events and others' actions.
2. Cells that fire together wire together. The more a child (or adult) engages their story neural net to interpret incoming sensory input, the more likely they are to do it in the future.
3. The evolutionary predisposition is reinforced by the dominant use of story throughout childhood. Children hear stories, see stories, have stories read to them and read stories themselves. This dominance of story exposure through the key years of brain plasticity results in adults irrevocably hard-wired to think in story terms.

The vivid visual imagery that good stories create in our minds stimulates our emotions, engages our interest and creates an environment in the brain that is conducive to learning.

TEACHING AS STORYTELLING

Egan's study of story-based learning led him to the discovery that children can readily understand abstract concepts when organised into story form. He writes about how from an early age children are engaged in constructing and understanding metaphors and forming images from spoken words. In his book *Teaching as Storytelling* (1988) he encourages us to see the curriculum as a great story that we need to tell rather than a series of learning objectives that we need to attain. Oral cultures use story, rhythm and rhyme to help them to remember a range of possibilities, as they have no recourse to other methods of recording their words.

Storytelling is fantastic tool for us to us to use to engage children, particularly when we are basing our work around such a strong theme as giants. A head teacher reported that she believed learning should be about creating a series of memorable experiences. What better way to create memorable experiences than through the method adopted by oral cultures throughout history, with its proven ability to enable us to retain information and pass it on to others? If we look back at our own schooling – perhaps particularly our mathematics education – what were the memorable lessons?

Storytelling has recognised the potential to create memorable experiences, but what is less recognised is the benefit of sharing stories with children in their early years for the development of mathematical ability. Canadian researchers have discovered that 'time spent on stories (telling, reading and listening to stories) during preschool years improves maths skills upon entering school . . . developing logical and analytical thinking as well as language literacy' (Haven 2007: 4, citing O'Neill, Pierce and Pick).

MATHEMATICAL IDEAS IN STORY FORM

But storytelling activities are not something simply to be left behind in early childhood. Trisha's personal engagement with mathematics was described, in Chapter 2, as being linked to her discovery of *Teaching as Storytelling* (Egan 1988). She was curious to test out Egan's assertion that you can teach anything, even mathematics, through story. Mathematics developed out of human experience (Cairns 2007) and stories developed out of the quest to learn more about mathematics (Berlinghoff and Gouvea 2004). Hughes (1986) reminds us of the way in which, in some languages, counting words themselves may tell a story – one as the moon, two as the eyes, seven for the apertures in the head and so on.

As soon as a mathematical concept is put into story form it comes alive. Egan (1988) argues for seeking out the powerful story behind every aspect of the curriculum since these will give purpose and meaning. The Canadian-based Imaginative Education Research Group (http://www.ierg.net) describes the use of story in engaging children. By accepting one penny for a chore on one day, doubling this fee on the second day and continuing to double the fee on each subsequent day children could quickly come into a serious sum of money – a story with great interest for them.

Kieran Egan (1988) has developed a framework for creating powerful stories. Key to what he believes a powerful story to be is the inclusion of what he terms 'binary opposites'. Traditional stories often include archetypal binary opposites such as good and evil; wealth and poverty. Table 6.1 is based on Egan's explanation of the ways in which the strong stories needed to fully engage the learner are best constructed.

The questions raised may be seen as fundamental to the education of children. Egan asks 'why should this topic be interesting for children?' This is an interesting

Table 6.1 Kieran Egan's story model form

1	**Identifying importance**	
	• What is most important about this topic?	Which aspect(s) of this topic could make it interesting to children?
	• Why should it matter to children?	What is it about the topic/subject which could make it matter to children?
	• What is affectively engaging about it?	What emotions or feelings might it be used to arouse in children e.g. sadness, envy, happiness, hopes, fears etc.?
2	**Finding binary opposites**	
	• What powerful binary opposites best catch the importance of the topic?	Children's learning is based on extremes e.g. *hot* and *cold*. Exploring these extremes enables them to develop understanding of the variations in between e.g. *warm*. For this reason we support learning by identifying the opposites relevant to this topic.
3	**Organising content into story form**	
	• What content most dramatically embodies the binary opposites, in order to provide access to the topic? • What content best articulates the topic into a developing story form?	The opposites identified should be used to create or identify a story which can illustrate them most effectively – taking the topic and opposites into account.
4	**Conclusion**	
	• What is the best way of resolving the dramatic conflict inherent in the binary opposites? • What degree of mediation of those opposites is it appropriate to seek?	Like all good stories this one needs satisfactory/satisfying conclusion. The focus on opposites means that there will have to be some resolution (or mediation) between them.
5	**Evaluation**	
	• How can one know whether the topic has been understood, its importance grasped, and the content learned?	How will we know that the children have increased their understanding of the chosen topic?

question to ask, and one rarely asked in education. However, having worked with teachers on exploring this model as a way of developing their approach to creative mathematics we have realised that, given the structured nature of the current curriculum, it is a question that many find hard to answer. Often their initial answer is simply 'because they have to know it'. It takes a great deal of digging sometimes to find out what is fundamentally interesting about some of the things that we require children to learn.

The case study below is taken from Egan's work (1988). It explores place value and was adapted by MakeBelieve Arts during our first exploration of story as a way of teaching mathematical concepts.

MATHS FOCUS ***A LITTLE OR A LOT* – BOOK 1, DRAMATIC MATHEMATICS**

- Place value
- Binary opposites: clarity/confusion, big/small

Scenario

The King of Sunobia boasts that his army is the largest. The King of Narcissus disagrees, and so the two armies gather on a large hill to find out who is right. But both armies look enormous. The kings try different ways of counting the armies, but they keep forgetting where they are. The numbers are just too large.

Finally a wise woman instructs three of the king's councillors to collect 10 pebbles and a wooden bowl. The soldiers then walk through a gap in a rock and as each soldier walks past, the first councillor places a pebble in his bowl. When the first councillor has run out of his 10 pebbles he empties his bowl, turns to the councillor on his left and says:

> I have no pebbles left. Can you put one pebble in your bowl to remind me what I have counted?

The second councillor puts a pebble in his bowl and the number 10 is established; one pebble in the tens bowl and no pebbles in the units bowl. The first councillor begins again, filling up his bowl and emptying it each time he has counted ten soldiers.

When the second councillor has filled up his bowl he turns to the third councillor on his left and says:

> I have no pebbles left. Can you put one pebble in your bowl to remind me what I have counted?

The third councillor puts one pebble in his bowl, the second councillor's bowl is empty, the first councillor's bowl is empty and the number 100 is created.

In this way all the soldiers are counted and at the end the third bowl has 9 pebbles, the second bowl has 7 pebbles and the third bowl has 4 pebbles. The king knows that his army consists of 974 soldiers.

continued . . .

MATHS FOCUS *A LITTLE OR A LOT* – BOOK 1, DRAMATIC MATHEMATICS . . . *continued*

Exploration

1 Children were given plates of uncooked rice to illustrate the difficulties counting large numbers. Each child was invited to count how much rice they had. At first the children began diligently trying to count the grains. Before long the enormity of the task overwhelmed the majority of them. 'It's too big,' announced one boy looking frustrated. The class was delighted to realise that it was ok that the task had beaten them.

2 Next they were given a second type of rice on another plate and left to explore how they could find out which pile of rice was the largest. Some of the children began pairing the rice in neat patterns. Some piled it up and tried to work out which pile was the largest. The enormity of the task again overwhelmed them.

3 Finally using the same approach as the councillor's, the children used pebbles and wooden bowls in 10s and units to find out how many children there were in their class.

Outcomes

- One school had groups of three children outside the hall at assembly time, counting in the pupils as they went through the door. The children counted as the kings had done using wooden bowls and pebbles. There were 327 pupils in school that day. One of the groups had a different number and they were able to identify where they had got confused.

Quote from evaluation

We learned counting and difficult numbers . . . You can count people when they go by one by one and put one pebble in the basket. At the end you can see how many there were by the pebbles, and you might only use a few pebbles to show a big number.'

Year 2 pupil

Further information

Using the pebbles, through this approach we were able to assess children's understanding of place value. We called out numbers which they had to make using their own set of pots and pebbles, e.g. 19 was formed by placing 1 pebble in the tens pot and 9 pebbles in the units pot.

The use of tactile objects like pebbles and wooden bowls was something the children really enjoyed as it tapped not only into their logical brain but into naturalistic intelligence. Children commented on the differing shapes, sizes and colours of the stones and enjoyed holding them and handling them.

References

Lee, T. (2003) *A Little or a Lot*, Book 1, Dramatic Mathematics Series, MakeBelieve Arts publication available from http://www.makebelievearts.co.uk.

Kieran Egan suggested this approach to exploring place value and it is written up as a lesson plan on http://www.ierg.net/lessonplans/unit_plan.php?id=26. You can also hear Egan and Calder talk about their work on http://www.youtube.com/watch?v=STOjZ7BeJw8.

Developing a story programme for children in the foundation stage, exploring numbers, was a challenge that resulted in us spending a long time trying to decipher what was fundamentally interesting about numbers. We kept coming back to the fact that counting and number are fundamental parts of what we need to be able to do. In order to begin to create a story using number we needed to find the excitement, the thing that would make it interesting to children, and not just something we as adults said that they should learn. It was only when we turned the question on its head and began to explore what a world would be like without numbers that we began to realise the full potential of the subject. The following case study is the result of our explorations.

MATHS FOCUS ***KING AND QUEEN OF NUMBER***

- *Counting:* forwards and reverse whilst marching around a room.
- *Number recognition:* identifying which number is missing in a line of numbers, and sorting numbers.
- *Emergent writing of numbers:* needing to write all the numbers on big pieces of paper to make sure we never lose the numbers again.
- *Problem solving:* thinking up solutions for how the world will cope without numbers.
- *Binary opposites:* clarity/confusion, lost/found.

Scenario:

In the Kingdom of Number the children are born each as numbers between 1 and 9. As soon as they are old enough they are sent to the palace of the King and Queen and drilled in lining up in numerical order and then in reverse order.

Once they are experts they fly out of their kingdom and into the world of the people where they stay, helping us with our counting. Until one day a mysterious storm arrives and the numbers are blown away. The people in the town don't know what to do without the numbers. They try to invent different ways of finding out how many there are of various objects by using sounds and physical shapes, but none of these methods are as good as the numbers they have lost.

Eventually the numbers fly back and the people fill the walls of the town hall with written numbers so if the numbers blow away again, they will never forget them.

Exploration

1. Children interacted with the story, inventing sounds and physical movements for each of the numbers. As this is a difficult concept they have as much fun in getting it wrong as they do in getting it right.
2. They played at shop, using sounds and actions to ask for the number of pencils or candles they need for a friend's birthday party.
3. They supported each other's learning by playing at being the numbers whispering answers to other children.
4. They helped to sort the numbers into groups when the wind brought them back in a jumble.

continued . . .

MATHS FOCUS ***KING AND QUEEN OF NUMBER*** . . . *continued*

5 They wrote numbers down on big sheets of paper to represent the walls of the town hall.

Outcomes

Children as young as 3 got very excited writing numbers on the town hall wall so that they would never be forgotten again. Even though some of the children were not confident in the shapes of the numbers they were writing, they demonstrated emergent writing, saying the name of the number they were making in a bid to pin them down in case they got blown away again.

Quote from evaluation

> I was amazed to see how excited the children were about writing numbers at the end of the session. They enjoyed the story notion that they needed to pin the numbers down in case they vanished again. I have witnessed boys who shy away from any written activity impatient to get a place at the lining paper wall in order to have their turn to make their mark.
>
> Nursery teacher

References

King and Queen of Number is a programme developed and delivered by MakeBelieve Arts (http://www.makebelievearts.co.uk).

EXAMPLES OF STORIES CREATED BY TEACHERS

One Year 1 teacher that we worked with went in early one morning and created a mess in his classroom to make it look as though it had been burgled. He then took some number cards and removed all the odd numbers. He then sprinkled the even numbers throughout the classroom, throwing them on the floor, on the desks, and throughout the room.

When he collected his children at the start of the day, he walked into the room and allowed the pupils to discuss what had happened. They discovered the number cards and tried to work out what might be going on. Suddenly one of them discovered a letter hidden on their chair. The letter was from Even Man, the great superhero and fighter for justice amongst all numbers. Even Man had been tracking Odd Man for several days now. Odd Man was trying to remove all the odd numbers from the world and the battle had now reached these pupils' classroom. Throughout the coming days pupils had to work with Even Man through a series of clues and adventures to find the odd numbers, and protect them from being whisked away again.

When we met up with the teacher after this work had taken place he was invigorated by the responses of his class to this activity. The excitement in this class around odd and even numbers had engaged all of the children and everyone understood the differences between the two, even taking time to hide all the reclaimed odd numbers at the end of each day, and packing them up to send on a holiday after their ordeal was over. Apparently the number 9 had a great time in the Caribbean!

Other teachers used shoes and a story about making a bed to fit a princess to explore standard and non-standard measurements, and another group created a person made out of shapes who wanted to discover the shape of the world.

Some of the stories worked better than others and the exercise was not easy. But the premise of using story to explore mathematics is an instant hit when it comes to engaging children. As a Year 4 pupil in the evaluation of a term-long story mathematics programme at her school reported:

> It's a really good way to educate children. I don't like maths; making maths into a story was great. I felt as though I wanted to do it . . . Maths is not popular and no way would I normally want to do it, but if I wanted to do it as a story then it must make it easier to learn for all children.

USING STORIES TO TAKE ON ABSTRACT IDEAS

Stories make things memorable, giving coherence to what may seem to be an unrelated set of ideas. This may be particularly true for abstract ideas since we do not have automatic mental images to support memory:

> The major processes of memory are the creation, indexing, storage, and retrieval of stories . . . We have great difficulty remembering abstract concepts and data. However, we can easily remember a good story . . . stories provide tools, context, relevance, and elements readers need in order to understand, remember and index the beliefs, concepts and information in the story.
>
> (Haven 2007: 71, citing Schank)

Algebra Stories

Another way that story can be used is to create algebraic formulas. Some children from Years 5 and 6 found this an exciting way into thinking about algebra. They were asked to:

> Look at the following equations and see if you can make sense of them:
>
> a) $1C + 1FG > 1SM + 2US$
> b) $1P + 5WM = \text{transportation}$
> c) $1HP + 1GS + 1C = H \infty A$
>
> If I tell you it is the story of Cinderella, does this help?
>
> a) 1 Cinderella and 1 Fairy Godmother are greater than 1 Stepmother and 2 Ugly Sisters

b) 1 pumpkin and 5 white mice equals transportation
c) 1 Handsome Prince and 1 Golden Slipper plus 1 Cinderella equals Happy infinity after.

The symbol for infinity might be more advanced symbolism than you would plan to explore with primary children, but when a group of children were involved in creating their own algebra equations for known stories a Year 5 boy asked if there was a symbol to represent forever. The teacher and children together searched on the internet and then realised that the infinity symbol was perfect. It soon appeared in many of the pupils' story formulas. Both children and adults alike engage with this way of recording either an aspect or the whole of a story using symbols. As a fun device after reading a short story or a chapter from a book one class we worked with created algebra equations that contain the main aspects of the plot.

Stories for memorising facts

Another use that story can be put to is for memorising numbers and formulas. Engage pupils in trying to create stories that will help them to remember the difference between mean, median and mode for example.

We have worked with several Year 5 and 6 pupils on creating stories to remember number properties. The eight prime numbers (2, 3, 5, 7, 11, 13, 17, 19) were remembered by one group through the following story:

> There were 2 elephants, who ate 3 buns and went to sleep for 5 hours. 7 dwarves arrived with 11 monkeys. They pelted the unlucky elephants with 13 bananas for 17 long minutes. 19 minutes later the dwarves and the monkeys were gone and the elephants were eating bananas.

It might not be the greatest story in the world, but because of the way our brains are hardwired to seek out narrative it works. We can imagine the annoying monkeys pelting the sleeping elephants with bananas and we fill in the gap between 17 minutes and 19 minutes where we assume something sinister has happened to the monkeys.

The story here is used to create a way of making sense of what is otherwise potentially a meaningless string of numbers. It is much easier to remember the story. Children added suggestions for ways to help reinforce their memory of the numbers. Thirteen unlucky bananas was the addition of one girl who was struggling to remember the number, but who knew the superstitious myths surrounding 13. Another child commented that how he remembered the 19 was by filling in the gap; he thought it was funny that the monkeys and the dwarves pelted the bananas for 17 minutes and then 2 minutes later they were all gone. We had great imaginary conversations about what happened to them in those two minutes. What the children above demonstrate in this process is how the brain is able to connect with story, and how narrative images expand in the brain, not only clarifying the gaps, but confining the information to memory.

CHILDREN'S STORIES

We should not overlook children's own stories, which are part of the process described in the last chapter of making it real for children. Below some work undertaken by children in a Year 2 class is described by the school's headteacher Jeannie Hughes:

> This learning came from the children's interest in football and the adult's observations of the children's play. The teacher followed the children's lead and used the context of football to teach a variety of skills in all areas of the curriculum, including a number of mathematical opportunities.

During the term the children were observed bringing football cards into school and spending a lot of time swapping cards, comparing scores, calculating points and discussing team places. The teacher wisely decided to extend this interest and use them as a starting point for learning in mathematics.

The teacher dedicated a display board in the classroom for the children to bring in photos and pictures of their favourite football teams, information about players, team places in different leagues and much more. On a Monday morning the children's favourite teams' results from matches at the weekend were calculated and discussed, with the teacher drawing on the mathematical learning possibilities. This scaffolding of the learning developed skills in mathematical vocabulary helping the children to see a purpose and meaning for learning and using mathematical language in context. The children's skills in calculating were developed through work on team points and points needed to improve league positions. Later in the term the children also developed their own teams and own football leagues extending the learning further.

The football cards interest was developed and extended and the children made their own cards developing complex scoring systems which were discussed and explored with the adults. There were opportunities to count, share and use probability. The teacher took the mathematical learning objectives for the half term and personalised the learning for those children who were particularly interested in this context, which were both boys and girls. The learning was very motivating and relevant for the children and helped develop our school's focus on cross-curricular learning and developing personalised learning opportunities.

This interest also influenced the parallel Year 2 class who were exploring an imaginary character called 'Bob' created by the children. Bob took over the whole curriculum. This class created the West Bobbers football team and the teacher abandoned the learning journey planned and developed the mathematical learning around this interest. Part of this included a 'Bob's bowling alley' invented by the children which the teacher used as a starting point for practical experiences of counting, scoring and calculation.

CHILDREN'S BOOKS FOR TEACHING (AND LEARNING) MATHEMATICS

In Chapter 8, we outline a teacher's story entitled *Farming for Fractions*. A children's book on a similar theme, but which raises some alternative and challenging ideas, is

Anno's Magic Seeds (Anno 1999). A book which, like the teacher's story, explores fractions is described by Whitin and Wilde (1995, xii). Sadly the book itself, *Tom Fox and the Apple Pie*, is out of print, but a child's comment on the power of the book, with its binary theme of fairness and unfairness is interesting:

> I wish my teachers had read math books to me. That's the first time I've ever really understood why the smaller bottom number is worth more (why 1/2 of a pie is larger than 1/8 of a pie, even though 8 is greater than 2 in whole numbers). Are there any more books that teach that math? I learn better that way.

In Chapter 7 we will explore the topic of giants about which any number of gripping stories have been written – encompassing as giants do binary opposites of huge and tiny, powerful and powerless. *Two Ways to Count to Ten* (Dee 1990) is a traditional Liberian story which, like many traditional stories, has its own power. *Six Dinner Sid* (Moore 2000) is a story which appeals to young children, but which has endless mathematical potential. A good rule of thumb is probably that if it doesn't grip you, it won't engage children.

Books about mathematics

There is, in contrast to stories which happen to address mathematics as part of our world, a plethora of books which set out to teach about mathematics. Here, we have selected a few which are interesting for a variety of reasons. There are many more which we have rejected for inclusion – sometimes because they are poor stories, sometimes because we don't happen to like them and sometimes because in our experience children haven't liked them very much. As we said in the introduction to this book, this is not a recipe – it is an invitation to take some risks, explore, push the boundaries and teach more creatively.

Here then are a few of our suggestions:

- *The Number Devil* (Enzensberger 2008) is what children often call a chapter book. The hero is 12 so that suggests that it is aimed at older children but some children still at primary school will be entranced by this 'mathematical adventure'.
- *Anno's Mysterious Multiplying Jar* (Anno and Anno 1999) has charming pictures and difficult ideas but is highly stimulating. The book involves 1 island, 2 countries, 6 mountains, 24 walled kingdoms, 120 villages, 720 houses and so on.
- *The Real Princess – A Mathemagical Tale* (Williams and Fatus 2008) gives a great mathematical twist to the story of the princess and the pea. Lovely illustrations and humour make it almost fit into the previous category of books – those with a story in their own right.
- *One Hundred Hungry Ants* (Pinczes 1993) is a short story which explores the different ways in which 100 ants can line up as they march towards a picnic. By the time they get there all the food has gone!
- *Spinderella* (Donaldson and Pichon 2002) is about football-playing spiders. Although published as part of the Banana reading scheme, the highly acclaimed

author Julia Donaldson has injected interest and humour into the story. It includes a maths game, some mathematical facts and ends with the cheer 'up with numbers!'

FURTHER READING

Brandon, K., Hall, N. and Taylor, D. (1993) *Math Through Children's Literature*. Westport: Libraries Unlimited Inc.

Haven, K. (2007) *Story Proof: The Science Behind The Startling Power of Story*. Westport: Libraries Unlimited.

Schiro, M. (2004) *Oral Storytelling and Teaching Mathematics*. London: Sage Publications Ltd.

Whitin, D. and Wilde, S. (1995) *It's The Story that Counts*. Portsmouth, NH: Heinemann.

CHILDREN'S BOOKS

Anno, M. (1999) *Anno's Magic Seeds*. New York: Penguin Putnam Books for Young Readers.

Anno, M. and Anno, M. (1999) *Anno's Mysterious Multiplying Jar*. New York: Penguin Putnam Books for Young Readers.

Dee, R. (1990) *Two Ways to Count to Ten*. New York: Henry Holt and Co.

Donaldson, J. and Pichon, L. (2002) *Spinderella*. London: Egmont UK Ltd.

Enzensberger, H. (2008) *The Number Devil*. London: Granta Publications.

Moore, I. (2000) *Six Dinner Sid*. London: Hodder Children's Books.

Pinczes, J. (1993) *One Hundred Hungry Ants*. New York: Houghton Mifflin Co.

Williams, B. and Fatus, S. (2008) *The Real Princess*. Bath: Barefoot Books.

CHAPTER 7

TEACHING MATHEMATICS CREATIVELY: GIANT MATHS

The world of giants and their interaction with humans is an incredibly strong premise on which to base not just one, but a series of maths lessons. The topic is so rich that it could be the subject of a whole term enquiry, bringing with it not only mathematics but also a range of cross curricular approaches, stimulating learning by involving children in a project with enormous possibilities. Children are fascinated by giants but so are adults. Myths, legends and folk tales are littered with extremes – giants and little people (see for example Allan 2009). These stories rest on binary opposites of huge and tiny; power and powerlessness; or perhaps guile and force. If you spend any time crouched down or walking around on your knees, at the same height as most of your pupils, you may get an understanding as to why. Everything that children look up at is gigantic compared to them. Adults and buildings tower above them. The idea of giants, taller than all they can see, is fascinating and immediately engaging.

Begin to create in a child's mind something as simple as a visual image of a giant's hand and immediately you enter into the world of mathematic possibilities. How much wider is the hand compared to one of our hands? How long are the giant's fingers?

Source material for this work can be found in numerous children's stories. The simple story contained in the book *The Giant Jam Sandwich* (Vernon Lloyd 1988) has the potential to act as a springboard into a world of exploration around many aspects of mathematics. The illustrations and rhyming text tells the story of a village plagued with wasps. To solve the problem of the wasps, the townspeople decide to trap the creatures in a giant jam sandwich, working together in a strange and imaginative way. The book can engage a class in a range of cross-curricular activities including cooking and exploration of quantities, size and scale, giving clear mathematical directions on how to make a sandwich to the possibilities of a science lesson on exploring the anatomy of a wasp. Just how much dough would be needed to bake a loaf of the size used by the villagers? How much would the ingredients cost?

Another great giant book that we have based a large proportion of our work on is the story of *Gulliver's Travels*, particularly focusing on Gulliver's adventures in Lilliput. This story is rich with mathematical possibilities. In the original version

Gulliver himself comments about the mathematical abilities of the Lilliputians, their capacity to build machines and use pulleys and ropes to haul him up off the beach, and their creative ability to solve problems using mathematical concepts:

> The emperor himself gave orders to have a bed prepared for me. Six hundred beds were brought in carriages. One hundred and fifty of their beds sewn together made up the breadth and length and these were four doubled . . .
>
> An imperial commission was issued out, obliging all the villages nine hundred yards round the city to deliver in every morning six beebes, forty sheep, and other victuals towards my subsistence, together with a proportional quantity of bread and wine . . . An establishement was also made of six hundred persons to be my domestics, who had board-wages allowed for their maintenance, and tents built for them very conveniently on each side of my door. It was likewise ordered that three hundred tailors should make me a suit of clothes after the fashion of the country.
>
> (Swift 1993: 21–3)

Suddenly, from a reading of the above, the mathematical possibilities that surround caring for a giant with all its intricacies open up a whole range of work for the adventurous and creative teacher. How much taller than us is the giant? How much food do we need to feed him or her? If our giant gets stuck down a well how much rope would we need to pull him out?

The last question might sound slightly surreal, but in one mathematics programme children were asked to imagine that the army had locked a giant down in a well to prevent him from leaving them. The townspeople, realising this was unfair, decided to set him free. They discovered that when the giant jumped, his hand was just one metre away from the top of the well, but how high could he jump? There was only one way to find out. The children jumped against a wall covered in lining paper and a mark was made to show how high their hand could reach whilst jumping, and another to show how tall they were when their hand was stretched up in the air.

When all the class had jumped and been marked on the wall, they created a graph of measurements showing the range for the class of how high a jump could be. An average was taken and this was used to estimate how high a giant, who was six times as big as them, could probably jump. Add this to the metre remaining at the top of the well and they had a close approximation of how big the well was. Next in threes they plaited a rope long enough and strong enough to free the giant. Weaving and plaiting in threes involved following a simple pattern of ducking and stepping over each other's pieces of string working out the best way to move together to strengthen the rope.

The amount of mathematical knowledge needed to solve this problem was greater than the assumed ability of this Year 4 age group. But the interest and motivation, the fact that they found out which child could jump the highest and what the average jump was for the majority of the class made the learning enjoyable and relevant. The need to solve the problem in order to right the injustice that had been wielded on the poor forsaken giant spurred the class on to finding solutions. Their engagement was evident throughout the session.

MANTLE OF THE EXPERT

The Mantle of the Expert (MoE) is a drama technique that was developed and refined by Dorothy Heathcote. It is based on the belief that children learn best if they have a relationship to the subject matter being covered that is more akin to that of an expert than a pupil. Heathcote believes that engagement in classroom drama is an essential part of children's learning and is vital if we are to enhance pupils' ability to connect with the curriculum.

In her book *Drama for Learning* (1996) which she co-wrote with Gavin Bolton, Heathcote analyses her work with a variety of age groups and discusses how the MoE approach empowers children through purposeful activities. The benefits of MoE are that it gives pupils the opportunity to work together to find solutions to problems, discussing how they will proceed, what is the best thing to do next and generally creating their own pathway through the learning.

As experts, children take on the role of someone who has a degree of knowledge and understanding in an area, but who needs to work on the problem with their peers to develop through practice the additional skills they require to solve this particular problem. Heathcote developed this methodology through a realisation that this is how adults learn in their lives; through gaining knowledge in real situations through day-to-day experiences and the demands that responding to these needs puts upon them.

Heathcote and Bolton believed that the 'Mantle of the Expert provides a centre for all knowledge: it is always experienced by the students in terms of the responsible human being . . . an *active, urgent, purposeful* view of learning, in which knowledge is to be *operated on*, not merely taken in' (1996: 32).

During MoE pupils take on many roles, for example; they might, as in this giant example, be an archaeologist or a mathematician. The relationship of the pupils to the very real jobs that they take on engages them in finding solutions from their own skill base. The cross-curricular potential and the ability of this work to touch on very real mathematical ideas is great. For more examples of lesson plans for MoE work, visit http://www.mantleoftheexpert.com.

With older pupils we have engaged them in making 3D props for a film about giants, organising themselves into a film company, creating short scripts that involve the use of at least one giant object discovered by a group of humans. Pupils were then tasked with making this prop, exploring scale and size and linking the work with design and technology to build an exact replica of the smaller human version. Once these were completed pupils had the chance to act out their stories. Using the drama technique 'Mantle of the Expert' (see box) the pupils were put in role as expert archaeologists and mathematicians and set the task of discovering the mathematical properties of the objects that had been made by other groups.

CROSS PHASE GIANT PROGRAMMES

The topic of giants does not have to be restricted to any one age range. We have worked with this theme with pupils from nursery through to pupils in Year 7. The case study below identifies learning opportunities developed in a primary school:

MATHS FOCUS ***A GIANT'S BIRTHDAY PARTY***

- Size
- Shape
- Proportion
- Scale
- Pattern
- Circumference
- Planning/handling data

Scenario

Long ago, the townspeople of Deptford adopted a giant from the Ministry of Giants. His name was Bigfoot and he helped around the town cleaning the windows in the tall buildings, fetching footballs that had got trapped on the school roof and rescuing kittens that had climbed up trees. The townspeople loved having Bigfoot living with them.

Then one day Bigfoot disappears. Everyone searches for him and eventually he is found, hiding in his cave, having pulled an enormous rock across the entrance. The townspeople try to reach him but he will not let them in. They try to persuade him to leave the cave, but he will not come out. So they write to the Ministry of Giants to find out what they can do.

An enormous letter arrives telling them they have been neglecting their giant. Did they know it was Bigfoot's 100th birthday? Had they ever given him his own plate and knife and fork to eat with? Did they ever let him have giant friends to visit from the neighbouring towns?

The townspeople feel very guilty and realised they had done nothing to thank Bigfoot for all his work. They decided to throw a Giant Birthday Party for him.

Exploration

1. This programme of work took place over a school day in a two form entry school and involved all the children from Nursery to Year 4.
2. The children were invited to put themselves in role as townspeople and imagine that they had adopted the giant Bigfoot and they now needed to prepare for a giant party.
3. Nursery and Reception were tasked with making giant food, papier-mâché sausages, ping-pong ball peas, and extra long string spaghetti – mathematics involved size, shape, proportion.
4. Year 1 were invited to make giant party hats for the five giants – mathematics involved scale, size.
5. Year 2 were responsible for designing the table cloth – mathematics involved pattern and scaling up.
6. Year 3 created the plates and cutlery for the giants – mathematics involved circumference, scale.
7. Year 4 were responsible for running the event, timetabling when everyone would place their contribution in the hall and for making a giant birthday cake – mathematics involved timetables, using maths in planning and organisation, scale and size.
8. Towards the end of the day pupils took turns to bring their class's contribution to the hall and lay them out. Once everything was set for a giant celebration, each class visited

continued . . .

MATHS FOCUS ***A GIANT'S BIRTHDAY PARTY*** . . . *continued*

the hall to explore the story, by viewing the finished product and enjoying the work of their peers.

Outcomes

- Pupils across all age groups readily engaged with the programme and talked about the giant's party for many weeks afterwards. MakeBelieve Arts still bumps into pupils two years later who remind us that they were involved in the project.
- Discussions could be heard in each classroom about how tall the giant Bigfoot must be, making comparisons with other tall objects, using a giant shoe and golden mean to estimate his height and using the language of maths to enable them to fulfil their role in the story.
- Many pupils, particularly from Years 3 and 4 asked if the giant was really coming despite the fact that we had made it very clear at the beginning of each project that this was a story.
- Teachers were impressed with how engaged their pupils were in the activity and how the maths that they were involved in suddenly had a purpose.
- The teachers from one school spent time after the children had left making the hall look as if five giants hadn't cleared up after a party. The children were very excited about this when they came in the next day.

Further information

When using story in this way, we are not trying to make the children believe the story is true. We are asking them to engage with the play of the story. When we work with children we very clearly inviting them to pretend that they are the townspeople and this is their giant.

References

A Giant's Birthday Party is a programme developed and delivered by MakeBelieve Arts (http://www.makebelievearts.co.uk).

Is it real?

When children ask if a situation or scenario is real we often ask them what they think. If they are not sure, we explore the idea of story. If we try to convince children it is real then our focus shifts from the play potential of a good story to a debate about what is real. This does not mean we cannot fully throw ourselves into the play like the teacher who created the morning after the giants' party. If you watch children at play, that play is very real, but it is real within the safe world of pretend. In the case study above we have described the questioning by children from Years 3 and 4. One child in particular, from Year 4, quickly approached a member of the team and said scornfully 'Giants are not real you know!' At the end of the day, doubt had crept in, the very same boy approached to ask if giants were really coming!

One teacher who had not realised the importance of pretend and that children buy into a story within safe parameters made the mistake of exploring the folk tale *Chicken Licken* which tells the tale of the sky falling down. She set up a drama activity where half the class reported to the other children that the sky was falling down, but she forgot to let them know beforehand that they were playing the story. With children in tears and frightened to go outside, she quickly realised her error.

From an early age children learn to both give and read play signals – facial expressions which are shared and which signify a play situation (see for example Smolucha and Smolucha 1998; Carson *et al.* 1993). Perhaps difficulties arise when children are unused to seeing particular adults, such as those in school, in a playful or imaginary role. This may occur when schools begin to introduce playful or dramatic scenarios. Children are skilled at reading play signals both amongst peers and in their play with adults. If these are being misread or missed, adults probably need to examine their own behaviour and approach.

RELATIVE SIZE

In exploring the relative size of a giant, children began to explore the relationships between different parts of the body. Children (and adults) can become fascinated by the relationships that emerge:

- One's arm span is equivalent to one's height. Children can test this out amongst themselves by stretching out their arms and getting two people to stand at their fingertips – thus marking the distance of the full span. If the first child then lies down in the space between the two others they will discover that they fit well into the space marked out in this way.
- A piece of string can be used to measure the breadth of the shoulders. This will prove to be roughly a quarter of the child's height. As one child said: 'The string on the shoulders . . . I thought it was amazing. I never knew my shoulder was a quarter of my body, I kept the piece of string – it's on my bedroom wall and I showed all my friends.'
- Roughly six times the length of a person's foot makes up the length of our bodies.
- The adult hand is the size of our face, (although we discovered that this is not true for young children whose heads are proportionally larger than those of adults).
- The size of a foot is equivalent to the distance between wrist and elbow – a fact that staggers many adults who cannot believe that their feet are that big.

There are countless other examples of how parts of our body divide equally into other parts and when they work they feel like a piece of magic being revealed to us. There is also a fascination from all age groups that these rules remain generally true whatever your size.

The golden mean or ratio

The famous image created by Leonardo da Vinci of Vitruvian Man (see for example O'Malley 2007) highlights many of these relationships. The interactive version of this image on the website http://library.thinkquest.org/27890/applications6.html makes it possible to highlight the rectangles of which da Vinci claims the body is made up. The image shows the relationship between armspan and height. It emphasises the relationship from foot to navel and from navel to head. Moving down the body it is also claimed that the gradually increasing rectangles that can be identified reflect Fibonacci's numbers – namely 1, 1, 2, 3, 5, 8 and so on. (*The Number Devil* (Enzensberger 2008) includes an excellent description of this phenomenon.)

Another interesting relationship to the golden mean, also drawn from ancient Greek thinking, is the claim that the human body is based around the number 5. It is widely suggested that five has particular importance because:

- we have five appendages to our torso: arms, legs, head
- each of these contains five appendages: fingers, toes, openings on the face (if you don't count the ears)
- we have five senses: sight, sound, touch, taste, smell. However this alleged 'fact' is said to have emanated from Aristotle (or possibly Plato who taught Aristotle but wrote nothing down). Since that time, a range of additional senses such as echolocation and proprioception have been identified.

Using the golden mean with giants

Using the properties they have discovered from their explorations allows children to begin to work out how tall a giant is just from having access to his footprint, or a hand print, or a piece of string showing the length of this shoulders. Add an in-role character to this scenario of an anxious tailor who has been given the task of measuring the giant for a suit. She manages to take a measurement of the shoulders but then the giant begins to get fidgety and she gets scared, and now she has to make a suit for the giant by nightfall and all she has is the one measurement. Immediately we can have an exploration of fractions, scale and measurements, using what we know about our own bodies to discover and mark out the proportions of the giant.

CONJECTURAL THINKING

In Chapter 1 we talked about how children need to be 'seekers and solvers of problems' (Claxton cited in Alexander 2010) and how mathematics does not always need to have one clear right or wrong answer. Since giants are probably not real, they provide excellent material for 'thinking outside the box'! When trying to find out the height of a giant, a class of children from Years 5 and 6 were placed into groups. Each group was given a metre long giant toothbrush and a normal sized toothbrush. The children were asked to find as many ways as they could to discover the height of the giant and to mark out a masking tape line from one end of the hall for each way they discovered. The children used a variety of approaches:

- Measuring the normal size toothbrush with their hand and discovering it was roughly the same size, so then measuring how many times their hand went

into the giant toothbrush and working out that the giant was 6 times bigger than them.
- Measuring the brush section of the normal toothbrush, finding out how many times the normal size brush went into the giant size brush, which was roughly 8 times and working out that the giant must be 8 times bigger than one of them.

These two different answers are both logical and both involve reasoning, and yet one giant taped out on the floor was much taller than the other. The children got very excited when they realised that neither answer was wrong or right, and that both were good approaches to take, but they struggled with the very obvious difference between the two lines. This opens up discussions about the facts we are given and how much is based on assumption. Two normal sized toothbrushes can vary immensely in shape and size and yet we assume that the giant toothbrush and the normal-sized (children's) toothbrush that we used were comparable. By challenging the assumption that mathematics must involve right or wrong answers we make it a more creative and interesting subject.

Changing scale – changing perspective

The potential of giant mathematics is truly gigantic. Within stories, giants can do anything at all. As we have seen there are endless possibilities. However, it is also interesting to imagine that we are the giants and to consider the scale of those who believe us to be giants. Suddenly rather than working with objects 6 times larger than themselves, pupils can begin to think about objects 6 times smaller or about the size of a shoe. If the giant is a child giant then the children can use their own feet as the example of scale. The questions that now begin to open up are if the people are as tall as our feet, how big are the plates or the cups that they use, and what would it be like for us to have to eat or drink from these?

ACTIVITIES AND LEARNING

The topic of giants is one of many subjects which actively engage children. Is this because they embody the binary opposites that Egan (1988) tells us are necessary for a good story? Is it because, being not real, they allow for conjecture and narrative? Or, are they in children's terms, so real that they have irresistible interest? Whatever the reason, in the course of exploring this topic with children, real tasks have led to engrossed interest and heightened learning. Excitement is essential to learning – it makes things memorable and changes the chemistry of the brain to make learning more effective (Eliot 1999).

Children readily remember making giant plates and food. They remember having to write in giant letters and make a giant envelope so that the letter would be large enough for a giant to read. They remember receiving a letter so tiny that they had difficulty reading it. When exploring the role of the Lilliputians (Swift 1993), actually collecting enough litres of water for a day's supply for a giant proved a challenging and memorable task. Giants are not the only things that excite and motivate children. Creative teaching demands that we go on finding the other interests and enthusiasms which can stimulate learning in the same way.

FURTHER READING

Allan, T. (2009) *Myths of the World*. London: Duncan Baird Publishers.

Heathcote, D. and Bolton, G. (1996) *Drama for Learning, Dorothy Heathcote's Mantle of the Expert Approach to Education*. Westport: Greenwood Press.

O'Malley, C. (2007) *Leonardo da Vinci on the Human Body*. London: Crown Publications.

Wyse, D. and Dowson, P. (2009) *The Really Useful Creativity Book*. London: Routledge (see Chapter 6 on the Mantle of the Expert).

CHILDREN'S BOOKS

Briggs, R. (1973) *Jim and the Beanstalk*. London: Picture Puffins.

There is plenty of potential for mathematical activities – measuring for glasses, false teeth and a wig. Links with communication issues – tiny books for which he needs glasses, the large note from the giant.

Dahl, R. and Blake, Q. (2001) *The BFG*. Harmondsworth: Puffin Fiction.

Perennial favourite with a focus on the feelings evoked by giants.

Donaldson, J. and Scheffler, A. (2002) *The Smartest Giant in Town*. London: Macmillan.

Again – plenty of potential for estimation, conjecture and measurement. How big would the sock need to be to make a sleeping bag for a fox, for example? How long would a tie need to be in order to serve as a scarf for a giraffe?

Dunbar, J. and Dunbar, P. (2005) *Shoe Baby*. London: Walker Books.

This is about a giant baby who uses his giant father's shoe as a boat, a car and a plane. Good potential for talking about sizes. Links well with drama stories based around the giant shoe.

Farley, J. (1997) *Giant Hiccups*. London: Tamarind Books.

A giantess lives peaceably until she gets hiccups which sound 'like a hundred dinosaurs falling out of bed'. What might that sound like? Finally the children decide that she must be hungry and make her a vegetable stew. How many vegetables would they need? How big would the pot be?

Herrmann, F. and Him, G. (1986) *All about the Giant Alexander*. London: Piccolo.

An old text, more wordy than the average picture book and therefore probably better for KS2 than KS1. Good pictures which highlight aspects of size.

Hughes, T. (2005) *The Iron Man*. London: Faber Children's Books.

Hughes, T. (1994) *The Iron Woman*. London: Faber Children's Books.

Ross, T. (2008) *I'm Coming to Get You*. Lonson: Picture Puffins.

The story focuses on the little boy's fear of a monster. Only in the final illustration does the reader find out that the monster is tiny. Excellent opportunities to discuss comparative sizes.

Swift, J. (1994) *Gulliver's Travels*. London: Penguin Popular classics.

Swift, J (1993) *Gulliver's Travels*. Bath: Parragon Book Service.

Vernon Lloyd, J. (1988) *The Giant Jam Sandwich*. London: Piper Picture Books.

Walker, R. and Sharkey, N. (1999) *Jack and the Beanstalk*. Bath: Barefoot Books.

Wilde, O. (1982) *The Selfish Giant*. London: Picture Puffin.

CHAPTER 8

CROSS-CURRICULAR TEACHING: MATHEMATICS AT THE HEART OF THE CURRICULUM?

An approach to primary education which involves cross-curricular study has been regarded by some people as a matter of fashion. The introduction of the national curriculum led many schools to focus on single subject teaching but, as both the Rose Review (Rose 2009) and the Cambridge Primary Review (Alexander 2010) affirm, curriculum areas or subjects need not shape the way in which teaching is organised. Both reviews maintain mathematics as an identified subject area or domain but highlight the importance of cross-curricular studies. As Rose (2009: 25) suggests:

> There are times when it is right to marshal content from different subjects into well-planned, cross-curricular studies. This is not only because it helps children to better understand ideas about such important matters as citizenship, sustainable development, financial capability and health and wellbeing, but also because it provides opportunities across the curriculum for them to use and apply what they have learned from the discrete teaching of subjects.

Rose adds that:

> This approach respects the integrity of subjects but lessens the rigidity of their boundaries. Among other things it encourages children and teachers to think creatively 'outside subject boxes'.
>
> (Rose 2009: 28)

We would go further. Children learn mathematical (and other) skills best, at the time when they need to use them in meaningful, relevant and real contexts. Basing mathematics teaching and learning on cross-curricular activity creates opportunities to set mathematical ideas and concepts in an environment where they have real purpose, relevance and meaning. By placing mathematics in the context of other areas of learning, children's understanding is enriched, challenged and affirmed. Just as talking about mathematics is more challenging than just hearing about it (see Chapter 4), so applying mathematics in a variety of contexts ensures that understanding is heightened and knowledge made more secure.

In order to leave *Mathsland* behind (see Chapter 3), teachers must address what Rose terms those 'important matters' and allow mathematics education to become part of the real world. This can best be done by exploring with children what the applications of mathematics are in their everyday lives. If mathematics is to become a more creative subject it must break through those 'subject boxes'. All too often teachers are happy to integrate the teaching of history and art, for example, but lack the confidence to break free from what Boaler (2009) terms the *ladder of rules* – which rule mathematics. Of course there must be room for both discrete and integrated teaching but at the moment the pedagogy for mathematics is somewhat skewed in favour of the former.

In this chapter we will consider, broadly in line with the recommendations of the Rose Review (2009), five areas of the curriculum (omitting, for obvious reasons, mathematics). This will include consideration of the role of ICT in supporting children's mathematical understanding across the curriculum. We think there is much merit in Alexander's (2010) suggestion that ICT should be seen as part of communication. However, in this chapter it is largely considered, in line with Rose (2009), as part of scientific and technological understanding.

UNDERSTANDING COMMUNICATION

The Cambridge Primary Review (Alexander 2010) refers to this domain as 'language, oracy and literacy' and suggests, as indicated above, that ICT should in the main be linked to communication. Under what Rose (2009: 76) terms 'essentials for learning and life' he lists four areas of mathematical understanding. Of these, three are directly about communication:

1. Represent and model situations in mathematics, using a range of tools and applying logic and reasoning in order to predict, plan and try out options.
2. Interpret and interrogate mathematical data in graphs, spreadsheets and diagrams, in order to draw inferences, recognise patterns and trends, and assess likelihood and risk.
3. Use mathematics to justify and support decisions and proposals, communicating accurately with mathematical language and conventions, symbols and diagrams.

Ideas such as representing, interpreting and interrogating, justifying and communicating are clearly important elements in this domain and ICT has an important role to play in this respect. The role of oracy, including drama, in supporting and developing mathematical understanding is a key strand of this book. Language was explored specifically in Chapter 4, while the role of story and dramatic play was considered in Chapter 6.

It has become popular to think of literacy in much broader terms than merely being able to read and write (Marsh and Hallet 2008; Kress 2003; Bearne and Wolstencraft 2007). Kress (2003: 1) suggests that current changes in the literacy needed by today's children will have 'political, economic, social, cultural, conceptual/cognitive and epistemological consequences'. He is not alone in this view. Bearne and Wolstencraft (2007: 2) argue that conventional approaches to literacy are not sufficient for the needs of tomorrow's citizens:

> Texts that children are familiar with – including computer games and hypertext – often follow a different structure from sequential narrative, instruction and explanation. Presentational software and websites extend possibilities for hypertextual composition and digital technology, with its facility for importing pictures and manipulating text, means that presentation of writing can be more varied, involving design features that paper-based writing does not allow.

Talk of visual literacy or computer literacy is commonplace. Emotional literacy has become a household term and in Chapter 1 we cited the OECD's use of the term 'mathematical literacy'. This argues for an approach to mathematics which goes way beyond structured, desk- (or carpet-) bound activities. It requires a full understanding of and engagement in mathematics – and this will undoubtedly require integration into other subject areas or domains.

Data handling as communication.

Clements (2004: 56) highlights data handling as a means of communication – finding ways to communicate what the data means. He writes that 'data analysis contains one big idea: classifying, organising, representing and using information to ask and answer questions'. He continues by suggesting that:

> After gathering data to answer questions, children's initial representations often do not use categories. Their interest in data is in the particulars . . . For example, they might simply list each child in their class and each child's response to a question. They then learn to classify these responses and represent data according to category.

By these means they develop ways of getting data to 'speak' to them. A simple example of this might be a survey about children's means of getting to school. In the early stages children will simply list names and write or draw beside them bus, car, walking etc. Over time they learn to cluster the names under a picture of a bus for example. Gradually the children can be represented by a block or plastic cube – the representation gradually being made more abstract, using picture graphs or bar graphs. This process involves written, spoken, graphic and digital representation, which in turn communicates in a range of ways.

The role of drama

Kress (2003) compares a print-bound world with the world of today, in which he believes images hold sway. He terms these 'world-told' and 'world-shown' perspectives. However, drama (which is inextricably linked to narrative) has a particular role to play. Rose (2009: 27) identifies drama as 'a powerful arts subject which also enhances children's language development . . . [and] enrich(es), say, historical and religious studies as well as personal development by exploring concepts such as empathy'.

While this is undoubtedly true, such a view limits unnecessarily the impact that drama can and does have. It fails to take account of the powerful role that drama has in bringing together the 'world-told' and 'world-shown'. Acting out a story both tells and shows – but it does more than that. It gives insight into what might be, by drawing on imagination. In so doing, it promotes the conjectural thinking essential to creativity and problem solving, including mathematical problem solving. Listening to a story, with or without images or props, requires imagination – as does drama. The actor has to imagine that he or she is someone else, somewhere else, in another time, in different circumstances. The audience must imagine that a white umbrella is a swan, that someone wearing roller skates is a train or that a crate with a cloth thrown over it is a house, a cave or a palace.

As we saw in Chapter 1, imagination is part of the mathematical process. It is the bedrock of the abstract thought which is essential to mathematical understanding. It is also where creativity enters the world of literacy (and literature) – and with cross-curricular studies can also inform and enter the world of mathematics. In the case study that follows, the teacher of a Year 4 class, that had had difficulty tuning into fractions, created a story which they acted out.

MATHS FOCUS *FARMING FOR FRACTIONS*

- Problem solving
- Fractions
- Division

Scenario

A wise old farmer decides he is going to take a long holiday and gives responsibility for managing the farm (consisting of one fruit field and one vegetable field) to his two sons. The brothers decided to take a field each and to grow two crops in each field.

A seed seller arrives and tells the brothers that if they buy seeds from her they will grow twice as many crops. A week later she returns with new seeds that will help the brothers grow twice as many crops again. The brothers are now growing eight different crops each. Getting fed up of his field, the oldest brother asks his sibling if he can have a quarter of the fruit crops, in return for one-eighth of his vegetables. The younger brother agrees and they rebuild the fences between the farm.

continued . . .

MATHS FOCUS ***FARMING FOR FRACTIONS*** . . . *continued*

The younger brother is happy until he realises that he had less crops. They agree to swap again; half of younger brother's field for two-eighths in return. As soon as the fields are divided they begin arguing again. When their father returns he is angry that his sons had not been able to manage the farm without arguing. Ashamed of themselves they begin to divide the 24 pigs. But what is the best way to do it?

Exploration

1. The children are invited to act the story out, marking the fields and the dividing fences with masking tape, string or playground chalk (if working outdoors).
2. As the fences between the fields change, marker pens, coloured string or coloured chalk is introduced to differentiate the new boundaries.

Outcomes

- Bringing fractions to life on a large scale can really help to engage children in exploring mathematical ideas. No longer does maths need to be an activity where children sit at their desks dividing circles with pencil lines.
- While working with smaller numbers sometimes helps children to understand or solve number problems in particular (see Chapter 3), many problems can best be understood by working on this larger scale. This gives children more scope for physical action and alternative 'ways of knowing'.

Quotes from evaluations

I was so inspired by the INSET and the idea of teaching maths through storytelling that I was determined to create a story to help my Year 4 class who were struggling with fractions. Once I got the idea it didn't take me that long to work into a lesson plan, but I have never had so much fun in a maths lesson. The children really enjoyed it too and they really got it. This is a powerful approach that I will definitely use in the future. I just need to think of a story to explain multiplication next.'

Year 4 teacher who created *Farming for Fractions*

Further information

We have found that by bringing fractions to life in this way we are able to engage children in more complicated mathematics than the curriculum would dictate for their age group. Year 2 pupils working on a similar division exercise were engaged in dividing up an island equally between everyone who staked a claim in it. These young children were able to consider how they might have one 32nd of the island. All of this took place on a large piece of lino shaped like an island and involved lots of discussion on how to divide equally.

SCIENTIFIC AND TECHNOLOGICAL UNDERSTANDING

In general it is clear that science and design and technology are the application of mathematics. The data that is collected from a scientific investigation often involve numbers. Their analysis may require pattern identification and the results will need to be presented in a way that is meaningful to an audience. Making something often involves accurate measurement as well as problem-identification and problem-solving strategies. The draft programme of learning (Rose 2009: 175) for scientific and technological understanding states that this area of learning:

> provides purposeful contexts for children to develop and apply mathematical skills, in particular number, measurement, graphing, data handling, interpolation and extrapolation and costing their own products. Children can develop their ICT skills by using ICT for capturing, organising and analysing data and presenting results; and for sequencing instructions to control events and products.

The exciting thing about the cross-curricular studies that are proposed here is that the integrity of the mathematics and the other subjects involved is maintained. In order to do real science you have to use real mathematics. In order to design and make something real and worthwhile, functional and aesthetic you have to use real mathematics. Construction will be explored further in Chapter 10 but it is an important aspect of cross-curricular activity – with a great deal to contribute to mathematical understanding.

A Sussex school undertook a food technology exercise. Children sought out recipes, cooked and sold cakes and biscuits. This involved:

- sourcing recipes which would not be too expensive
- increasing recipes to make sufficient for sale
- shopping for ingredients
- counting, calculating, weighing and measuring to make the items
- estimating a price which would be acceptable to the buyers but would still provide some profit.

Over time and through discussion and investigation, they modified their approach. They decided to sell some fruit and vegetables, as a healthy option, and they undertook surveys to determine what kinds of cakes and biscuits were most popular. Most of this work relied on mathematical understanding but in carrying it out, mathematical understanding was enhanced because there was a context. The work was real – with tangible outcomes and benefits.

Similarly work in Years 5 and 6 on scientific enquiry requires mathematical understanding and application. Planning the enquiry involves problem-finding as well as problem-solving strategies. Gathering data, explaining results and considering evidence all involve mathematics. This is, by its nature, a cross-curricular area of study.

ICT

It is beyond doubt that mathematics and ICT have many close links. Programmable toys such as Bee-Bot; Roamers and Pixies offer mathematical opportunities at different stages of development and expertise. Multi-modal work, based around sound, images and robotics, is both supported by and supports a great deal of mathematical thinking and understanding – time, planning, sequencing and so on.

With the development of new technologies, such as augmented reality programs, the full potential to link ICT and mathematics has perhaps yet to be realised. Holding a card with a picture of a car on it in front of a computer fitted with augemented reality programming will result in an image of yourself holding the paper, with a three-dimensional car in your hand. Touch a green box on the paper you are holding and the car changes colour. Touch another box and the car spins around. Another box activates the seat storage and immediately you can see how much storage room there is in the car you are thinking of purchasing. (To view videos of augemented reality on your computer visit http://demos.t-immersion.com/.)

Although the technology is in relative infancy, augemented reality software that explores geometry and allows pupils to examine three-dimensional images from pieces of paper containing an outline of a shape are already in existence, and the capacity of this technology to create incredible new uses for ICT in the future promises to get stronger. The reality of this is summed up in the powerful video short *Did You Know We are living in Exponential Times?* (YouTube. http://www.youtube.com/watch?v=lUMf7FWGdCw). The video suggests that technology is enabling us to become more global, and states that 'We are currently preparing students for jobs that don't yet exist, using technologies that haven't been invented yet, in order to solve problems we don't even know are problems yet'.

The Rose Review (2009) commissioned a separate report from Becta (2009) on ICT in primary schools. Becta (2009: 77) suggests that children in the primary school should:

- Find and select information from digital and online sources, making judgements about accuracy and reliability.
- Create, manipulate and process information, using technology to capture and organise data, in order to investigate patterns and trends; explore options using models and simulations and combine still and moving images, sounds and text to create multimedia products.
- Collaborate, communicate and share information using connectivity to work with and present to, people and audiences within and beyond the school.
- Refine and improve their work, making full use of the nature and pliability of digital information to explore options and improve outcomes.

All of these skills will develop in combination and lead to:

- Understanding: using modelling visualisation and real life experiences to develop deeper knowledge and appreciation of subject concepts and complex ideas.

While these, the *what* children should learn, are all capabilities which we would wish children to develop, the *how* is more contentious. Alexander (2010: 269) challenges Rose's view that ICT should be seen as a 'skill for learning and life' and suggests that ICT is in danger of becoming 'a tool without apparent substance or challenge other than the technical'. He continues by arguing that ICT should be seen primarily as an aspect of communication. This he suggests would:

> enable . . . schools to balance and explore relationships between new and established forms of communication, and to ensure that the developmental and educational primacy of talk, which is now exceptionally well supported by research and evidence, is always maintained.
>
> (Alexander 2010: 270)

Alexander (2010) is by no means alone in urging caution. There is such a groundswell of popular support for more time and resources to be spent on technology that it may require some creative or 'out of the box' thinking to consider some alternative points of view.

Neuroscientist Susan Greenfield (2004) urges caution. Her evidence to the Cambridge Primary Review team is cited by Alexander (2010: 270). She warns that:

> The mid-21st century mind might almost be infantilised, characterised by short attention span, sensationalism, inability to empathise and a shaky sense of identity . . . If the young brain is exposed from the outset to a world of fast action and reaction, of instant new screen images flashing up with the press of a key, such rapid interchange might accustom the brain to operate over such timescales . . . Real conversation in real time may eventually give way to these sanitised and easier screen dialogues . . . It is hard to see how living this way on a daily basis will not result in brains, or rather minds, different from other generations.

More than a decade ago, Healy (1999) was voicing similar concerns about children's use of ICT. She argues that children need kinaesthetic activity and real-world experience. Over-reliance on technology will not build 'intelligent muscles'. It is all too easy to develop (and to choose or purchase) software which produces convergent rather than divergent thinking. This is particularly true in mathematics, where as we have seen, there is already an over-dependence on the one-right-answer approach. While some children may gain from some practice sessions with lists of sums, this can and should never replace practical experience and opportunities to discuss and justify answers both to complex problems and to simple computations. The excitement of appearing to hold an apparently three-dimensional augmented reality car (which moves and changes colour as if by magic) in the palm of our hand should not persuade us that concrete practical experience is no longer necessary.

A third major area of concern which teachers concerned to address the need for a curriculum for the twenty-first century should be aware of is commercialism. Much software (and indeed hardware) relies on heavy and highly influential marketing. Twenty-first-century teaching should be alerting children to this manipulation of choice and decision making. Blind and uncritical use of technological resources which involve such influences should be used with great caution. Although it may have many other applications, augmented reality software, for example, is being developed for marketing purposes. In using ICT we need to ensure that children have the critical powers to deal with market influences. Creative approaches to mathematics can give children the skills they need to identify problems, to categorise and to analyse.

HISTORICAL, GEOGRAPHICAL AND SOCIAL UNDERSTANDING

Alexander (2010) proposes some parallel but different domains of learning from those suggested by Rose (2009). These include citizenship and ethics; faith and belief; as well as place and time. Devlin has suggested that mathematics might be taught more successfully as an aspect of human culture – in which case much of it could be subsumed into this domain of learning! (See Chapter 10 for more information on this topic.) Rose (2009: 167) suggests that cross-curricular studies involving both mathematics and this area of understanding might involve 'creating timelines, using plans and maps and using data to analyse a real problem in the community'. The case study below develops mathematical understanding through the device of a Tudor market.

In Chapter 7 we considered the drama technique known as the Mantle of the Expert, which has enormous mathematical potential. As highlighted earlier in this chapter, Rose suggests that drama is helpful in developing historical understanding. In one history topic, pupils were put in MoE roles as placement checkers responsible for Second World War evacuation procedures from London to Essex. The pupils were involved in map making of the village of Little Heddington, recreating the map in three-dimensional form from the information they had about the village. They also needed to create criteria for checking the people who had agreed to take evacuees, sort out which children should go to which houses, whether boys of girls would be more suitable for one house than another and make sure that all the children had somewhere to go. Alongside this pupils were engaged in a range of other activities, making decisions about people's suitability to have an evacuee, writing their memories of the trip for a national newspaper and deciding on their values as a team with the responsible role of re-housing children.

Although this was essentially a history topic, through dramatic engagement, the pupils became involved in large amounts of mathematical thinking – including gathering and presenting data and problem solving. The process of turning language-based information into a three-dimensional image also has mathematical implications to do with distance, space, ratio and area.

UNDERSTANDING PHYSICAL DEVELOPMENT, HEALTH AND WELL-BEING

There are any number of mathematical applications arising from physical and fitness activities – either in competition with others or in improving personal performance. Similarly, a developing sense of well-being can be enhanced through the way in which

MATHS FOCUS ***TUDOR MARKET***

- *Fractions and percentages*: all the special offer labels require groups to work out the new price of the goods they are purchasing and selling.
- *Problem solving and strategic thinking*: creating a scenario where there is no right or wrong approach, and where pupils need to think about how cheaply to sell their goods to encourage buyers but also consider how not to make a loss.

Scenario

The Lord of the Manor is holding a competition to find the most enterprising stall owners in the land and he invites the children to set up their stalls, create a name for their shop and price their goods so as to attract the most buyers. He announces that there will be a prize for the person who earns the most money.

Exploration

1. The children are divided into groups and given an area of the room in which to set up their market stall. Each stall sells exactly the same products as the other.
2. The products are the types of thing you would see in Tudor times: a pig's head, a cup and ball etc. All the prices the children are given to sell the goods at are in Tudor Crowns, and they are exactly the same price for each group.
3. Each group is then given the same number of special offer labels that enable them to reduce the price of some of their goods. The labels can state that this item is half priced, or has a 20 per cent discount etc.
4. The groups have to decide in secret which items to give the discounts to. Do they place it on the item that is the most expensive, or will that mean that they will lose potential income on a sale? When they have decided they place their discount cards and reveal their stall to the rest of the room.
5. Each group is given a shopping list of items they must purchase from other stalls and have time to wander around to find the best deals. Lists are kept of who purchases what from whom and at the end of the first round the amount of money made by each stall holder is noted.
6. The pupils then have time to discuss if they need to change which items they discount for the second round.

Outcomes

- Often pupils try to sell the most expensive items without a discount, but the group that first takes the risk of lowering the price of this item soon discovers that more people want to shop from them.

Quote from evaluations

> The children really enjoyed this sophisticated version of playing shop, and began to get more and more tactical with each round.
>
> Year 5 teacher

Further information

This idea can be adapted to fit any period in history. It is also possible to extend the approach to explore Enterprise Education in a modern day context.

mathematics is taught. A conjectural, problem-solving approach, collaboration and discussion can all help to enhance a child's sense of self.

An understanding of the role of physical action in mathematical development is rarely considered yet brain studies show an increasing awareness of the interdependence between brain and body (Blakeslee and Blakeslee 2007). Dramatic mathematics, acting out mathematical scenarios and stories with a mathematical focus, can give children a different perspective. It offers an alternative 'way of knowing' (Claxton 1997). Gardner's theory of multiple intelligences (1999) emphasises the interrelatedness of different intelligences. There is long-standing evidence of the impact of spatial awareness on mathematical understanding (Clements 2004), the numerical aspects as well as those more expected elements concerning shape, space and measures.

Kinaesthetic mathematics

Mathematical ideas can be explored kinaesthetically as part of a more physical approach to the subject. Simple techniques of throwing balls around the class to get answers to different mental maths problems can add an urgency and speed that adds a dimension of fun. Standing all the children in two lines and getting them to pass a clap as fast as they can from the front of the line to the back, and then changing this to calling out the numbers of one of the times tables, one at a time from the front of the line to the back, can add a different dynamic that can put the fun back into lessons for children who need a more physical approach. This team approach often results in children supporting each other in remembering which answer they have to call out and played regularly can help to remind children of their tables.

Table 8.1 is an example of a physical response to learning number properties that was developed by MakeBelieve Arts as a revision exercise for Year 6 pupils. The chart was written on the board and various numbers were called out to the class. As soon as they heard the numbers they needed to respond with all of the appropriate actions that the specific number required.

For example if the number 80 was called out the class responded by rolling their hand, raising their left arm and then raising their right arm and finally by standing up. On the other hand the number 29 would only get a clap and an oooh.

Inviting a class to create physical shapes for plus, minus, equal, division and multiplication can be used to solve simple sums written on the board that are missing the necessary signs to make them make sense. Thus presenting children with three

Table 8.1 Example of a physical response to learning number properties

Even	roll your hand
Odd	Clap
Multiple of 5	raise left arm
Multiple of 8	raise right arm
Multiple of 10	stand up
Prime Number	say oooh

numbers such as 3, 6 and 18 would involve them in adding the movements for multiply and equals.

Another example of this type of work developed by MakeBelieve Arts was the creation of a Number Property assault course where Venn and Carol diagrams were used in a relay race to engage children in answering sums, finding the answer in a Carol diagram where they were sorted into odds and evens, under 20 and over 20, and then running with the number to a Venn diagram taped out on the floor. On arriving at the Venn diagram pupils have to place the number in the correct circle as to whether it is a multiple of 10, 4, both or neither.

The following comments are taken from students' evaluations of their kinesthetic work on mathematics:

- People think because it is maths you can just sit down and listen and we need it to be more interactive. We learnt so much more when we had the chance to get up and try things out (Year 7 pupil on a kinaesthetic maths lesson).
- Most of the time maths is boring. I like moving and learning and we don't do any of it, if we could learn maths through PE lessons it would be much more fun (Year 6 pupil).
- I still remember the (physical) sign we made up for divide. It was really cool. I learnt which way you do brackets and multiplication and I still remember it (Year 6 pupil).

These young people are clear about the benefits of physical action to their learning. However, one of the difficulties that faces teachers is the perception of others. Sometimes the children themselves are resistant to change, and following some kind of practical maths session will ask 'when are we going to do our maths?' This may be because working with pencil and paper feels safe and secure but it may also be because children know that their parents recognise what they are doing, as they are seated at a table, as mathematics. It may also be because they perceive the ambivalent attitudes of teaching and support staff themselves.

UNDERSTANDING THE ARTS

There is often a confusion between the creative arts and creativity. Central to this book and to the series is the idea that the arts do not have a monopoly on creativity. However, the creative arts do have a particular role to play in creative mathematics. The role of story and drama have already been considered but these and other forms of art all have a symbolic function. Pound (2008, 82) writes:

> Stories – whether published, told by children or created by adults – can be developed in a number of ways. The telling and retelling of stories may involve dramatic play (both formal and informal; large scale role-play or involving small world figures), music and dance, paintings and drawings, models and sculptures. The process of translating ideas from one creative medium to another supports children's thinking.

As we have seen, mathematics is an abstract subject. This means that it requires symbolic underpinning – a means by which we can think about it. This may be provided through imagination – dramatic play and exploration of story, and these aspects are addressed in Chapter 6. It may come about through discussion and collaboration as we saw in Chapter 4, but it is essential if children are to fully understand mathematics, exploring ideas and concepts creatively (Devlin 2000; du Sautoy 2004).

Music and mathematics are closely linked (du Sautoy 2004) and this will be explored more fully in Chapter 11. Brandt (2009) describes music as time in the mind, while du Sautoy (2004) suggests that music is internalised counting. Music – songs and rhymes – also creates representations of numbers in counting games and songs, rendering the number names more memorable. The government initiative *Sing-up* (http://www.singup.org) advocates singing as a fun way to teach maths!

Both two-dimensional and three-dimensional art activities develop children's mathematical understanding in many ways. Three-dimensional art will be explored further in Chapter 10. Drawing and play with three-dimensional figures and models can 'offer powerful tools for expressing complex ideas' (Anning and Ring 2004: 117). Anning and Ring (2004) go on to emphasise the narrative thread that runs through both forms of play as children explore and seek to understand the world – including the mathematical world.

We cannot however leave this aspect of cross-curricular work without thinking about the mathematics involved in Vasconcelos' giant model, made from saucepans and lids, of Marilyn Monroe's shoes (see http://www.christies.com/LotFinder/lot_details.aspx?intObjectID=5289859). They measure approximately 3 by 4 metres – and are stunning and exciting. There are many other sculptures and models that offer similar mathematical stimulation such as Italian artist Neri's 10 metre high table and chair. (For discussion of the world's largest chair see http://www.roadsideamerica.com/set/CIVIchair.html.)

The importance of mark-making

Worthington and Carruthers (2006) advocate an approach to young children's mathematical mark-making which they describe as 'bi-numerate'. By this they mean that children have to learn to represent ideas not just in oral language but to develop an understanding of the way in which mathematical ideas can be represented in secondary symbols. Teachers can support this process by understanding:

> the importance . . . of translating from one language (or creative medium) to another. Representing (or re-presenting) ideas verbally, graphically, in imaginative play or block-building enables children to think and re-think their ideas.
>
> (Pound 2008: 85)

The government document entitled *Mark-making matters* (DCSF 2008) also focuses on the importance of graphic representations of young children, highlighting the importance of encouraging:

> children's mathematical mark making (which) often arises spontaneously through a need to communicate in a meaningful context. Through their marks, children's thinking becomes visible and practitioners then gain valuable insights into their developing understanding of complex concepts. When children are asked to record, after they have finished a practical mathematics activity, motivation and meaning are often lost. Recording may then lack in-depth quality of thinking and is more like copying. Children's mathematical graphics are their own personal response to meaning making and involve deep levels of thinking. It is important that children make links between the spoken and written representations.
>
> (DCSF 2008: 42)

Hughes' (1986) findings that many children at the end of primary school still did not know how to use symbols mathematically lies behind this emphasis on mathematical mark-making. The children had been taught to use symbols but not to apply them to practical situations. Fortunately the primary national strategy advises against the early use of formal symbols. This stage of experimentation with symbolic forms should not be rushed since it is where the foundation of understanding and using conventional symbolic forms lies.

Matthews (2003: 1) underlines the way in which children use anything and everything to symbolise their thinking:

> Drawing especially helps the child's understanding of symbols, and signs and representation, understanding which will become crucial in her encounters with symbol and sign systems in home and school, and in the expanded world of literacy she will enter when she leaves school. This means that, in actions they can make with their own bodies, and in actions they can perform upon objects and media, but perhaps especially with drawing and painting media, children learn how to form representations, symbols and signs. This forms the basis for all thinking. If you think this through, this means that, far from being at the periphery of education . . . art has a central role to play in cognitive development. To think otherwise is a 'fundamental misconception'.

ICT, narrative and symbolism

'Digital literacy' (Marsh 2005), also involves children in symbolism and narrative. Smith (2005: 111) considers both 'play at the computer' and 'the use of computers for play'. In the first, she suggests, the development of play is similar to that with any other materials or equipment. She also suggests that computer use supports what she terms 'abstract transformation' (citing Vygotsky). Smith continues 'the ability to use and understand symbolic representations in one context can then be transferred to another context' (2005: 114).

In relation to the use of computers as props for office, space travel or home play, Smith cites research (2005 citing Labbo *et al.*) which suggests that 'using the computer as a prop at play centers [*sic* – meaning areas of provision rather than a setting] resulted in expanded symbol use, keyboarding skills, understanding of computer processes, and increased vocabulary' (Smith 2005, 111).

One important way of countering any harm that might come from the use of digital images is the growing and exciting practice of enabling children to make their own videos. Software currently available puts this well within the reach of children as young as 3 years of age. Nixon and Comber (2005) describe video-making with young children using video footage of the children themselves – but perhaps even more exciting is the production of animated sequences using soft toys, plasticine figures or Lego constructions. These have the advantage of demonstrating to young children how these visual representations are actually made. This in turn gives a great sense of empowerment.

Upitis *et al.* (1997) describe a relatively low-tech version in which a group of 8- and 9-year-olds create an animated film. The authors highlight the 'visual, mathematical, and musical potential' of the activity but indicate that of even more importance is the memorable experience itself and the impact it will have on their mathematical experiences later. They write:

> Where do ideas about rates of change, velocity, rotations, cycles and continuity (involved in trigonometry and calculus) come from? . . . [I]n this animation project, they have begun to grapple with a particularly fertile situation: one of a large number of 'real-world' situations where these ideas are fundamental.
>
> (Upitis *et al.* 1997: 77)

IS IT CROSS-CURRICULAR?

There have in the past been many criticisms of cross-curricular work. As Upitis *et al.* (1997) remind us it involves much more than doing sums on pumpkin-shaped paper because it's Halloween. Such an approach adds nothing, only detracts from mathematics, art and cultural understanding. They suggest that a truly integrated curriculum involves fluid movement from one area to another. Language, biology, ICT and mathematics were all involved in the animation project – learning in all these areas was enhanced through integrated and creative teaching.

FURTHER READING

Anning, A. and Ring, C. (2004) *Making Sense of Children's Drawings*. Maidenhead: Open University Press.

Sedgwick, F. (2002) *Enabling Children's Learning Through Drawing*. London: David Fulton.

Upitis, R., Phillips, E. and Higginson, W. (1997) *Creative Mathematics*. London: Routledge (see Chapter 3).

CHILDREN'S BOOKS

Fox, D. (1998) *People at Work: Making a Film*. London: Evans Bros Ltd.

Wenzel, A. (2010) *13 Sculptures Children Should Know*. London: Prestel.

CHAPTER 9

MATHEMATICS OUTDOORS: THE WORLD BEYOND THE CLASSROOM

The outdoors provides us with the space and many opportunities to teach mathematics in creative and enriching ways. By not only taking mathematics outside but also acknowledging the wonderful world of mathematics to be found in nature and in constructed buildings and artefacts, we encourage children to see mathematics as relevant to them and their world. The context may be the outdoor classroom, the neighbouring streets, the garden or the seaside. The development of forest schools and a flurry of writing about outdoor classrooms (see for example http://www.outdoorclassroom.org and http://www.ltl.org.uk; and *The Outdoor Classroom,* Harriman 2008) has heightened, or perhaps more accurately, reflected a growing interest in the importance of outdoor provision across the curriculum.

Outdoor provision is important for a host of reasons. In a Learning through Landscapes publication entitled *Mathematics in the School Grounds* Rhydderch-Evans (1993: 7) writes:

> School grounds present opportunities for making children aware that mathematics is 'real'. Wonder a little about the number of leaves on a tree or bricks in a wall and before you know it you'll be comparing and finding difference, adding, subtracting, multiplying and dividing. Plan to improve that space outside, perhaps by putting a few flower tubs here and there, and you'll soon be asking how much for this and that and the mathematics of economics will be staring you in the face. Make careful records of all your transactions and you will soon have more than enough data to work with.

The booklet offers some useful ideas for both Key Stages 1 and 2. It suggests that the aspects of mathematics most readily addressed outdoors are problem solving; investigation; mathematical discussion and communication; selecting appropriate mathematical tools or instruments for data gathering or problem solving and the consolidation of learning. It is suggested that this includes estimation, measuring, calculating, collecting and representing data and recognition of shapes and patterns.

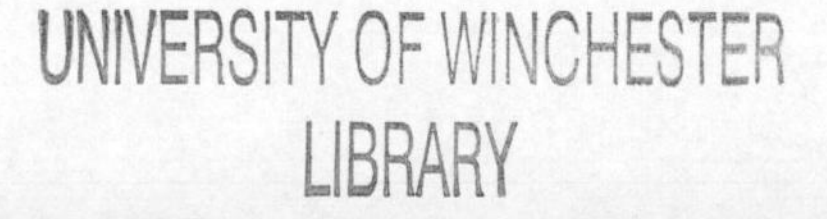

Perhaps the most important thing that children learn is that mathematics is actually part of the real world – not something to be done in school (or *Mathsland*).

A primary school in Deptford, south-east London, was funded by the local Heritage and Environment Trust to enable them to work with a designer and consultant on a whole-school approach to school grounds development. The programme engaged pupils from Foundation Stage to Key Stage 2 in planning, mapping and digging to transform their school grounds from an empty tarmac playground with a grass field at the back, into a nature reserve, pond and stimulating games areas including sheltered cover and seating areas. The mathematics involved in such a project was significant. Reception children needed to count how many sections of wall there were in the divide between their playground and the older children's section so that they could construct their own design for the walls. Classes in Key Stage 1 were involved in mapping the tarmac playground and dividing it into sections so they could decide which area of the playground the boat they had designed should be placed in and how this would fit alongside the painted games boards they wanted marked out in various sections. Pupils at Key Stage 2 submitted drawings for the pond and walkways that formed part of the nature reserve, measuring and calculating the desired size of each to ensure that all their needs were met. Alongside this planning stage, children were involved in the painting, digging and for some children brick laying that formed part of this incredible construction. Following on from this the school won £5,000 as a prize from Learning through Landscapes. Children from the school council were then involved in working out the budget to enable future grounds development.

TEACHING MATHEMATICS OUTDOOR CREATIVELY

Table 9.1 (pages 104–5) highlights the importance of outdoor provision and links it to both mathematical understanding and the development of creativity. The characteristics of outdoor play shown in the left-hand column are drawn from a book about young children and outdoor provision. Sadly despite the recent Manifesto for Learning Outside the Classroom (http://www.lotc.org.uk), most writing about outdoor provision focuses on the early years. While it is true that young children need space for active play, it is also true that everyone benefits from being outdoors – in terms of health, cognition and well-being (Louv 2006). In this chapter we hope to demonstrate that learning will not suffer but can become richer and more stimulating by being taken outside.

The outdoor classroom may be thought of in three distinct categories, namely the natural world, the built environment and the potential of what is sometimes called the outdoor classroom – the space available to the school. This may be its playground, playing field or community space.

CREATIVE MATHEMATICS AND THE WONDERS OF NATURE

Weather and natural phenomena offer experiences with mathematical potential which can only be accessed outdoors. Snow, rain, shadows all offer opportunities for

LEARNING OUTSIDE THE CLASSROOM MANIFESTO (LOTC)

> We believe that every young person should experience the world beyond the classroom as an essential part of learning and personal development, whatever their age, ability or circumstances.
>
> (DfES 2006a, front cover)

Launched in 2006, the Learning outside the Classroom Manifesto developed through advice and input from many experts with experience in this field (http://www.lotc.org.uk/Out-and-about-guidance/Introduction). The document is based on an understanding that learning outside the classroom is a vehicle for developing children and young people's capacity to learn. It stresses the importance of focusing on *how* and *where* children and young people learn, rather than primarily on *what* they learn. 'Experiential' or 'authentic' learning through experience has the potential to re-engage children with learning, making it relevant to them in their lives. Having the opportunity to explore their environment taps into the natural curiosity of children and young people to understand the world and their place within it. The potential to engage with learning, to collaborate with others, to and make new discoveries that learning outside the classroom creates are all highlighted in the manifesto as the reasons it needs to play a role in children's education. The document highlights learning opportunities:

> The potential for learning is maximised if we use the powerful combination of physical, visual and naturalistic ways of learning as well as our linguistic and mathematical intelligence.
>
> (DfES 2006a: 2–3)

It also identifies five areas where this type of learning can take place:

- School grounds
- Immediately outside the school
- Local but needs transport
- Day visit with transport
- Overnight stays

The growing interest for learning outside the classroom and the fact that the manifesto was created in partnership with experts, deliverers and the DfES is a clear indicator of how seriously this approach to learning is being taken and how important and beneficial this type of learning can be for children. The urgent need to improve the teaching and learning of mathematics (Boaler 2009) means that innovative and exciting opportunities for exploring mathematical ideas are worth examining.

exploration and investigation – the data from which can be represented in a variety of forms. Natural places like beaches and forests, meadows, rivers and hills hold not only mathematical potential but interest for children. Simply being outdoors and away from the school environment is exciting but to be there, as part of a community of learners, is stimulating. To return to the same place as the seasons change the environment gives not only an enhanced sense of wonder but greater insight into the nature of pattern and time.

Table 9.1 The benefits of outdoor provision for the development of creative mathematics

The importance of the outdoors (Tovey 2007: 37–8)	The benefits of outdoor provision for the development of creative mathematics
Space and time to try things out	Spatial and temporal understanding are crucial mathematical concepts – perhaps best understood in an outdoor context. A psychological sense of space and time is provided by time spent outdoors. It is claimed by Cobb (1977) that the 'inventiveness and imagination of nearly all of the creative people she studied was rooted in their early experience in nature' (Louv 2006: 93).
An environment that can be acted on, changed and transformed	Transformation is important to the development of creative thinking, including mathematical thinking. This ability to change the environment leads to the flexible thinking which underpins both creativity and real mathematics.
A dynamic, ever-changing environment that invites exploration, curiosity and wonder	Exploration and curiosity drive the problem-solving approach to mathematics (Boaler 2009). Exploration, curiosity and wonder are the driving force behind creativity.
Whole body, sensory experience	Human learning incorporates many 'ways of knowing' (Claxton 1997) including the physical. Clements (cited by Pound 2008) underlines its value, writing that 'children's ideas about shape do not come from passive looking . . . they come as children's bodies, hands, eyes . . . and minds. . . . engage in action'.
Scope to combine materials in ways that are challenging Opportunity to make connections in their learning	The essence of creativity lies in making unusual connections. Making unusual connections relies on an ability to think flexibly which in turn comes from experience of putting unexpected things or ideas together either physically or mentally.
A rich context for curiosity, wonder, mystery and 'what if' thinking	Problem-solving and creativity rely on a 'what if' mentality – conjectural thinking.
Space to navigate and negotiate the social world of people, friendships; to experience disagreement and resolve conflicts with peers	Collaborative interaction and discussion are essential to good problem solving. This means that children need to learn how to 'navigate the social world' if they are to get the most from such opportunities.
Opportunity for giddy, gleeful, dizzy play	Excitement is difficult for teachers since most classes involve large numbers of children but it is excitement which leads to effective learning (see for example Eliot 1999). Enthusiasm and 'ecstatic responses' (Egan 1991) are an easily recognised part of creative activity but more difficult to reconcile with mathematics since that is so often taught in a passive, sedentary fashion – but creative mathematics demands that we make space for excitement about mathematics.

continued . . .

Table 9.1 *. . . continued*

The importance of the outdoors (Tovey 2007: 37–8)	The benefits of outdoor provision for the development of creative mathematics
Potential for mastery, a willingness to take risks and the skills to be safe	The risk-taking associated with outdoor provision normally involves physical risk, while the risk-taking generally associated with creativity is more to do with psychological risk. This may not involve physical injury but it may reveal anxieties about getting things wrong. An approach to mathematics that relies on problem-finding and problem-solving requires learners to take risks.
A wide range of movement opportunities that are central to learning	Marcus du Sautoy (2008: 15) describes movements central to his fascination with pattern: 'I can't ignore the strange pattern that adorns my swimming trunks. Even footsteps in the sand get me thinking about a problem that I can't stop exploring once it's occurred to me. How many different ways can I mark out shapes in the sand as I make my way along the beach? My simple footsteps are something called a glide reflection – each step is got by reflecting the previous footstep then gliding it across the sand. Now I hop along the beach kangaroo-fashion, and my two feet create a pattern with simple reflection. When I spin in the air and land facing the other way, I get a pattern with two lines or reflectional symmetry. In all, I manage to make seven different symmetries in the sand.'
Experience of the natural world and understanding of their own place within it	In the evening, on the same beach (see previous row) du Sautoy (2008: 31) asks himself some questions: What's the strange mix of physics and biology that gives me the sensation of seeing the shimmer on the waves? . . . Why are there two high tides a day rather than just one? . . . Science progresses because of the questions we can't answer. Without unsolved problems to work on, mathematics would die. Children's questions may (or may not) be less profound but the sense of awe and wonder engendered by nature can have an equally profound impact on learning and creativity.
Opportunities for learning in all areas of the curriculum	Outdoors learning offers wide opportunities for cross-curricular activity. Mathematics linked to science, games, design and technology and geography are but some of the more obvious possibilities.

Zac, a Year 2 pupil, attends a small school. The school have an allotment which they tend, and in it, something which is called the secret garden. In addition, the whole school goes out on a seasonal walk through local woodland and common ground at fixed points in the year. Zac's family have a garden where they too grow vegetables. They walk regularly, rain or shine, in the surrounding countryside. So the experiences which the school offers are not new but they are important to Zac – they are seen as if they were new because he goes in the company of different adults and different children. This sense of seeing things through new eyes is an important aspect of creativity – even, as can be seen from Marcus du Sautoy's description (see above) of his time on the beach, in relation to mathematics. It may be that this new perspective is particularly important in mathematics education – a subject which for so many has lacked any context or sense of wonder – a subject only to be found in *Mathsland*, not in the real world.

The natural world of animals and plants also offers mathematical opportunities for creative learners and teachers. Sampling numbers of buttercups and daisies on a field of grass in order to estimate total numbers or average per square metre is a great experience for a sunny afternoon. Identifying and describing the patterns to be found in leaves and flowers offers opportunity for mathematical discussion. The habits and habitats of animals provide any number of mathematical opportunities, from devising humane fox or squirrel deterrents to collecting and presenting data on the bird population of a particular environment.

There is a wonderful book entitled *Actual Size* (Jenkins 2006). It contains beautiful life-size drawings of a range of animals (or parts of animals – depending on their size). On the first page, for example, there is a picture of an atlas moth, at 30 centimetres 'so large that it is often mistaken for a bird'. Comparisons between this and the native butterflies of this country have enormous mathematical potential. So too does the fish on the same page, a dwarf goby, at just 9 millimetres; and the giant Gippsland earthworm at 90 centimetres. The eye of the giant squid is also 30 centimetres. A wonderful activity can arise from this – marking out the size of the giant squid, whose body and tentacles are 18 metres long. This book provides the kind of information that children of primary school age find so riveting in the *Guinness Book of Records*. Such wonders intrigue children and can be the starting point for many mathematical questions and investigations.

The work of the artist Andy Goldsworthy makes use of natural materials – stone, wood, ice, leaves, thorns and petals. The images he creates are full of mathematics. A French book *Artistes de Nature* (Pouyet 2006) is of great interest to children, portraying as it does natural materials used to create interesting images and objects. The mathematics of quantity, shape, space, geometry and algebra can be found and developed. Similarly the artist Richard Long produces what is sometimes termed Land Art. In this time and distance, as well as shape, become important.

CREATIVE MATHEMATICS AND THE EVERYDAY WORLD

Mathematics in the built environment may be equally diverse. In addition to mapping exercises, which will be explored in the next chapter, traffic surveys, shopping expeditions and educational visits can all provide mathematical and creative learning opportunities.

Andrews and Trafton (2002) describe planning a trip to the zoo. Five- and six-year-olds are trying to work out how many coaches they will need. The authors give a detailed description of the discussion and processes of representation the children go through in trying to solve the initial problem of how many people will actually be going on the trip. They arrive at an answer of 52 children and the driver and then have to work out how many adults will be needed – and therefore what the final total will be. The numbers they are working with are large but the problem is real and they persist. The authors suggest that 'young children can engage in substantive problem solving and in doing so develop basic skills, higher order thinking skills and problem solving strategies' (NCTM 2000: 103, cited by Andrews and Trafton 2002).

Older children working on a similar expedition may work out costings, food allocations and timings. Picnics, journeys to the coast, educational visits to museums or theatre, or even camping trips can be used to develop similar but perhaps more complex problems and investigations. As we saw in Chapter 3, even very young children can use a range of strategies for working out real and meaningful problems. Children can work out the money involved, schedule the timings of events and itineraries, decipher timetables for public transport and so on. The possibilities are endless – what so often prevents us taking on the activities is concern about coverage or the prescribed curriculum. As was pointed out in Chapter 3, children learning mathematics through a creative problem solving approach do at least as well as others and often better.

CREATIVE MATHEMATICS IN THE SCHOOL PLAYGROUND

Being outdoors in the school playground, garden or playing field makes it possible to make more noise, make more mess, or work on a larger scale than being indoors, and this offers greater potential for mathematical learning. It also offers access to things which can only be done outdoors – such as weather investigations. This might involve checking rainfall or wind direction. It might be about plotting the movement of shadows or finding the height of a tree. The importance of these things for a creative approach to mathematics should not be underestimated.

Messy maths might include gardening or simply digging mud. A group of Year 6 children were learning about negative numbers. In order to explore this concept the children were invited to dig holes in the soil to represent negative numbers, fill them to ground level to represent zero, and create small humps for positive numbers (see http://www.channel4.com/programmes/dispatches/4od#3057301). The concept of messy maths might also include the use of water. Long lengths of guttering provide stimulating collaborative work and taxing problem-finding and problem-solving opportunities as children work together to find ways to make water run uphill and down dale. Where's the maths? It lies in thinking about angles, heights, distance and capacity. The mathematical understanding lies in discussion during the task and reflective review afterwards.

The space offered by outdoor environments opens up lots of potential for creative mathematical activity. Even relatively small outdoor areas can give a sense of space – which can be quite liberating. The space provided by being outdoors can be used for drawing out dinosaurs of given dimensions – or giant squids! The question 'if that tree were cut down, in which direction do you think it should fall?' would involve finding the height of the tree and measuring the spaces around it. (For details of tree measuring see for example http://kidsactivities.suite101.com/article.cfm/measuring_big_trees.)

On a relatively mundane, but still stimulating level, outdoor space gives opportunities for ball games, skittles and other competitive activities such as races, skipping, obstacle courses and so on. In addition to the mathematics involved in scoring and timing, children may become involved in devising leagues and statistics. The methods of representation and the effectiveness of the presentation of data is every bit as vital an aspect of mathematics as the sums involved.

Mathematical challenges and environments

School playgrounds can also be used to create specific environments for the development of mathematics. Treasure hunts can be devised with a mathematical slant. Nick Butterworth's *Treasure Hunt* (2003b) might provide a starting point. Children from Years 5 and 6 might make up clues for younger children or, as happened in a London primary school, parents worked together with their children. Depending on the age of the target audience the clues, which could be recorded on a hand-held recording device or written, might include:

- The next clue will be found 18 × 3 adult paces due north of this point.
- Facing the school's cherry tree, turn 90 degrees to the right and, when you reach the climbing frame, turn 90 degrees to the left.
- Count the daffodils in the green window box and take that number of paces towards the bench.
- This clue will be found beside a number 46.

Children in the reception class might be supported on a mathematical challenge by older children. Rhydderch-Evans (1993) suggests that reception class children are helped to understand positional language by being asked to 'stand between the'; 'sit on top of the' or 'go around the'. The interesting thing about this challenge is that the older children are also challenged. They are asked to devise a game for the younger children in which there isn't a muddle of children all trying to do the same thing at the same time.

Maths trails might include an angle hunt – locating right angles, acute angles, exterior angles and so on. Alternatively they might focus on different kinds of symmetry (Rhydderch-Evans 1993). Skinner (2005) suggests a number of different kinds of trails – footprint trails, a number hunt, a pattern walk or an obstacle course. She also suggests a photographic trail – something which older children would enjoy creating for younger children or, working in teams, for one another. It could be complex, involving many different aspects of mathematics, or it could be relatively simple, using photographs of mathematical features of the local environment. Children could simply be asked to find out where, for example, a particular green square or gold 42 was to be found.

The Secret Path (Butterworth 2003a) would also be a good stimulus for setting up a maze. Strictly speaking, mazes are multicursal – and labyrinths unicursal. In other words it is not possible to get lost in a labyrinth because there is only one path, while mazes, like the one at Hampton Court, offer a number of choices. Nowadays the words are often used interchangeably. Children are fascinated by both types and could be encouraged to set some up outside using posts weighted down in large tins with concrete and flexible fencing or plastic sheeting to create the barriers, or simply by chalking the outline.

Wyse and Dowson (2009) describe work with eight-year-olds, based around the subject of Theseus and the Minotaur. Their focus is not mathematics but it is creativity.

MATHS FOCUS ***A RIVER ALWAYS FINDS ITS WAY – BOOK 4, DRAMATIC MATHEMATICS***

- Positional and directional language

Scenario

The wicked witch Avara hears about Lily's magic with numbers and decides to kidnap her and lock her in a tower surrounded by a maze. When Prince Zecko discovers a message from Lilly concealed in a bottle he knows he has to rescue her, but can he find his way to the tower?

Exploration

1. The children are put into pairs and one of them is blindfolded. Their partner has to give positional and directional instructions to them to enable them to navigate an obstacle course that has been created either outside in the playground or in the school hall. They are involved in moving over and under objects and part of the instructions they are given must include the precise number of paces forward etc.
2. A maze is chalked out on the playground and the class have to work together to give one child who is blindfolded the instructions they need to reach the middle.

Outcomes

- The children got very excited about the maze and this work was extended to involve them in creating their own mazes which were subsequently marked out in the playground.

Quote from evaluation

Directional language can be difficult to demonstrate but this session used excellent practical exercises and also problem solving, i.e. a maze that had to be escaped from, to teach. The children loved this practical and game-like context and the fact that we could do it outside added to this enjoyment. The session really helped the children to understand. It made learning their left and right much easier. The session was well paced and the work was pitched for everybody.

Year 2 teacher

Reference

Lee, T. (2003) *A River Always Finds its Way*, Book 4, Dramatic Mathematics Series, MakeBelieve Arts publication available from http://www.makebelievearts.co.uk.

What it does is draw out the emotional aspects – what a labyrinth means in real life terms – rather than simply a paper exercise. In the case study that follows, a maze (or more properly a labyrinth) was created. Children responded emotionally because they cared about the heroine of the story.

Den-building

Very young children build dens out of blankets and armchairs, cardboard boxes and net curtains. But dens are attractive to older children too. Tovey (2007: 75) reminds us that 'den making seems to be a feature of middle childhood' in many countries and cultures. Children's literature is full of examples of children creating secret small spaces and most people have some memory of making a den somewhere. Of course, there are many reasons related to children's personal, social and emotional development that make sitting under your gran's table for hours on end seem attractive, but there are mathematical reasons too. The more we have watched young children (and even some older ones) cram themselves into boxes, the more apparent it becomes that this activity has something to do with measuring oneself up against a visible amount of space. When we took a giant size shoe into school as part of the work on giants, the first thing many children in Year 4 wanted to do was to get inside it. Indeed when rehearsing for a show, even the actors wanted to get inside it! 'That's how much space I take up' seems to be the thinking that is going on at every level. This need to explore physical ways of knowing should not be underestimated (Claxton 1997; Gardner 1999).

Many mathematical problem-solving activities can be undertaken in relation to den-building or children, given the right materials, will find problems. Of course, an outdoor environment offers the most scope but this kind of construction can go on indoors as well. If they can be developed in a space in which they do not have to be dismantled every day but can evolve this too may be an advantage (Knight 2009). Questions like those listed below, either posed as a problem-solving activity or emerging from children's play in response to their problem-finding, could nurture both creative and mathematical activity:

- How many people could fit in this den?
- How can we make this shelter big enough for four more people?
- How can we make this strong enough to withstand the wind but light enough to transport to the forest?
- How big will the floor space have to be to accommodate 4 sleeping bags?
- How can we fit a table and chairs into this space?

Tovey (2007) cites research which indicates that richer play occurs in dens with ceilings; a number of connecting 'rooms' or spaces; different ways of entering and exiting; and from which children can see out without being seen. This indicates a problem sufficiently challenging to engage even adults – so cannot realistically be seen as too babyish. White (2008: based on page 119) suggests a wide range of materials and resources which can support den-building. These include crates, tyres, large hollow blocks (from Community Playthings), real bricks, large cardboard boxes (both presented as 3D boxes and flattened out as 2D nets), large plastic flower pots and plastic drums, water barrels etc., guttering, carpet rolls and plastic piping of different lengths and thicknesses together with plumbing joints with which to connect them, bamboo canes and Build-a-Ball connectors (designed for making fruit cages but perfect for constructing shelters etc.), planking, plastic-coated mesh fencing, clothes airers, large pieces of fabric including curtains and blankets, tarpaulin, camouflage net and plastic sheeting, carpet tiles, beach mats or similar, ropes and pulleys, joining materials such as gaffer tape and bulldog clips.

We can hear teachers, used to teaching mathematics at desks or on the classroom carpet, gasping in horror at this list. You may well be asking 'where will we store this stuff?', 'who will tidy it up?' and 'how will I know what they are learning?'. All we would say is try it! Experience the children's excitement. Listen to their insights and, in turn, gain insight into their creative thinking. We will return to many of these issues in Chapter 12 of this book.

The team work and collaboration which comes from this kind of work is of vital importance. In Chapter 4, the role of collaborative discussion in enhancing mathematical competence was explored. The learning which comes from group exploration of a more physical nature is also of great importance. One other point to make is that smaller and more manageable materials such as twigs and pebbles (White 2008) can be used to work on miniature versions of similar ideas. Paradoxically, although in Chapter 3, the problem-solving strategy of 'trying a smaller case' was suggested, in this case smaller may not be similarly helpful. You have only to think of the wobble on Norman Foster's Millennium Bridge over the River Thames to realise that small constructions do not always reveal the true nature of the problems thrown up by the reality of a larger replica.

FURTHER READING

du Sautoy, M. (2008) *Symmetry: A Journey into the Patterns of Nature*. New York: HarperCollins Perennial.

Lonegreen, S. (2001) *Labyrinths*. New York: Sterling Publishing Co. Inc.

Louv, R. (2006) *Last Child in the Woods*. New York: Algonquin Books.

Rhydderch-Evans, Z. (1993) *Mathematics in the School Grounds*. Winchester: Learning through Landscapes/Crediton: Southgate Publishers Ltd.

Tovey, H. (2007) *Playing Outdoors*. Maidenhead: Open University Press.

CHILDREN'S BOOKS

Butterworth, N. (2003a) *The Secret Path*. London: Collins Picture Books.

Butterworth, N. (2003b) *The Treasure Hunt*. London: Collins Picture Books.

Jenkins, S. (2006) *Actual Size*. London: Frances Lincoln Children's Books.

Pouyet, M. (2006) *Artistes de Nature*. Toulouse: Editions Plume de Carotte.

Steer, D. (1996) *Mythical Mazes*. Andover, Hants: Templar Books.

CHAPTER 10

BUILDING MATHEMATICAL UNDERSTANDING: CONSTRUCTION AND ARCHITECTURE

In this chapter we explore the relationship between construction, architecture and mathematics. We will examine the mathematical potential of examining architecture and examine the mathematical and creative possibilities of block play and other construction materials. Blocks are sometimes regarded as only appropriate to the early years of schooling. As noted in the previous chapter, many of the references are to young children but this is only because relatively little work of this type has been done with older children. We hope that this chapter will convince you that these materials and activities are banished from the classroom far too early, long before their potential for mathematical learning has been exhausted.

ARCHITECTURE

Architecture and mathematics have historically been linked since ancient times. In classical Greece and Ancient Rome, architects were also required to be mathematicians. The construction of the pyramids is testimony to the mathematical theories that surround their creation. Unlike Devlin who declares that 'maths is not about number but about life' (see Chapter 1 of this book), Pythagoras believed that 'all things are numbers' (http://www.thebigview.com/greeks/pythagoras.html). His views were taken up by Plato who held the view that architecture had greater aesthetic value than flowers. He loved the straight lines and circles that could be created by builders and architects but were not replicated in nature. Greek buildings such as the Parthenon were based on a ratio known as 3:4:5. Building to this ratio produced right angles as well as proportions which classical thinkers regarded as pleasing to the eye (Berlinghoff and Gouvea 2004) (see Figure 10.1).

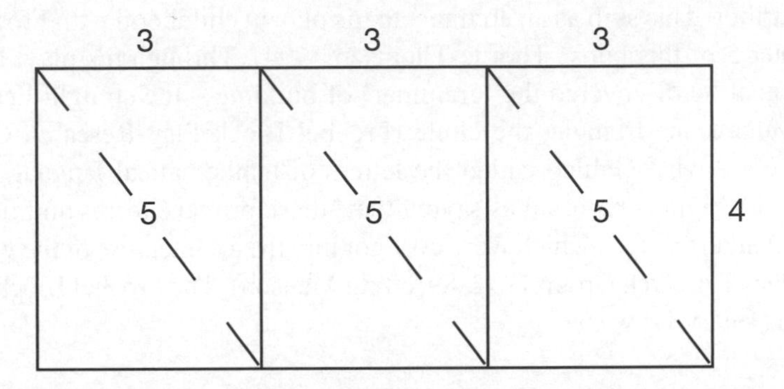

Figure 10.1 3:4:5 Properties pleasing to the eye

The Egyptians had known that a triangle whose sides are in the ratio of 3:4:5 would be a right angled triangle and Pythagoras built on this knowledge to develop his famous theorem (Berlinghoff and Gouvea 2004) (see Figure 10.2).

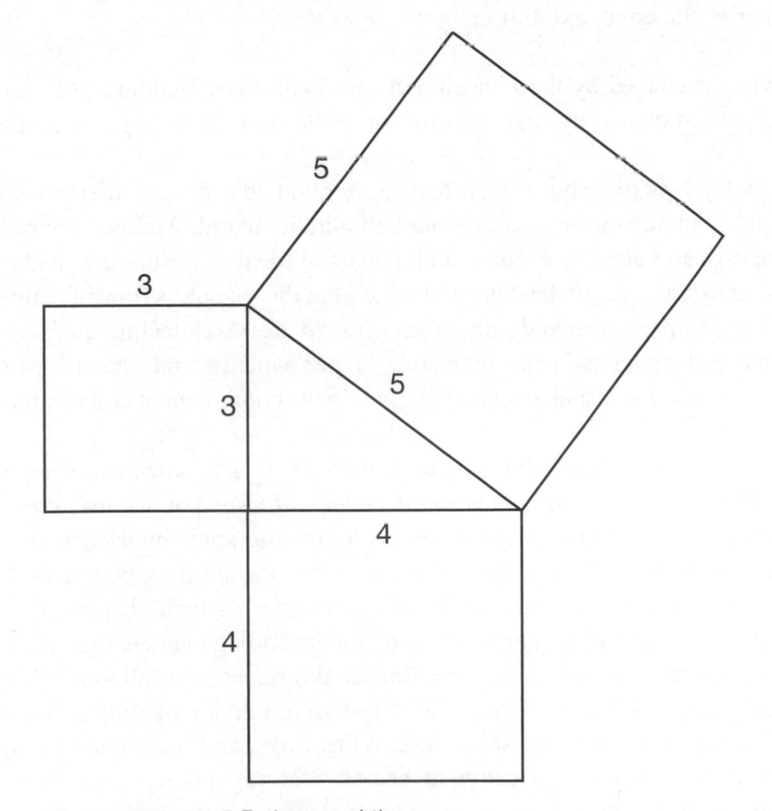

Figure 10.2 3:4:5 Pythagoras' theorem

The Golden Ratio formulated during the Renaissance period by Fibonacci involved a rectangle measuring 2 × 3³⁄₁₆ inches. For Fibonacci, these measurements conformed to 'relationships found within the natural world' (Read 1992: 8). Frank

Lloyd Wright attributed his skill as an architect to his play in childhood with Froebel's Gifts (see Chapter 5 of this book; Thorne-Thomsen 1994). Through his play, Lloyd Wright claimed that he discovered the 'grammar' of building – the straight line, the flat plane, the square, the triangle, the circle (Froebel Block Play Research Group 1992: 89). These are what Galileo called the letters of mathematical language (see Chapter 4). Lloyd Wright is reported as saying that 'these primary forms and figures were the secret of all effects . . . which were ever got into the architecture of the world' (Froebel Block Play Research Group 1992: 89, citing Manson). The Froebel Block Play Research Group (1992: 89) writes:

> A fine example of the fusion of mathematics and aesthetics is the Guggenheim Museum in New York, designed by Wright, which consists of a gently spiralling interior ramp rising from a base of a mere one hundred feet in diameter and yielding over a quarter of a mile of continuous display space for works of art . . . This has been described as one of the most magical spatial experiences . . . At any moment one is in intimate proximity to a small group of works yet in the presence of the entire exhibition.

This view is echoed by the Finnish architect Pallasmaa. Buildings are as much symbolic representations as any other construction. Pallasmaa (2005: 71) reminds us that:

> The timeless task of architecture is to create embodied and lived existential metaphors that concretise and structure our being in the world. Architecture reflects, materialises and eternalises ideas and images of ideal life. Buildings and towns enable us to structure, understand and remember the shapeless flow of reality and ultimately, to recognise and remember who we are. Architecture enables us to perceive and understand the dialectics of permanence and change, to settle ourselves in the world and to place ourselves in the continuum of culture and time.

Architecture is closely related to mathematics. There are some interesting books aimed at children, such as *13 Buildings Children Should Know*; or *See Inside Famous Buildings*. However, children are also interested in photographic books depicting the work of Gaudi with its intricate shapes and patterns or the startling geometric forms of Libeskind. Drawing these and other buildings, discussing their shapes and forms gives another 'way of knowing', another way of understanding mathematics. Although not architecture in the conventional sense, Rachel Whiteread's installation of 14,000 white plastic boxes, which was based at Tate Modern in London in 2005/6, had many architectural features. It explored space in striking ways, and undoubtedly inspired many children and adults who came to see it – giving greater awareness and understanding of shape and space.

Creating replicas of famous architecture with cardboard boxes

Inspired by Rachel Whiteread's work, a Year 6 class were given a large supply of cardboard boxes and asked to consider how they could set about building replicas of famous monuments. The children looked at pictures of the Eiffel Tower, the Taj Mahal, Big Ben, Buckingham Palace and a number of other famous buildings. In groups they were given 10 minutes to use the boxes to create their own large-scale representation of these buildings. The children took the work really seriously and some amazing representations were created. The exercise worked as a fun introduction to exploring architecture and having the opportunity to recreate structures on a large scale. Pupils noticed the symmetry present in the pictures they were trying to recreate and the language used by the class to describe what they were trying to achieve in this simple activity was highly mathematical. The class teacher commented 'we had been looking at symmetry as a class, but I was surprised at how articulate the children were about this when they shared their constructed replicas with the class'.

BLOCKPLAY

> The child can certainly be interested in seriating for the sake of seriating, and classifying for the sake of classifying, etc., when the occasion presents itself. However, on the whole it is when he (sic) has events or phenomena to explain or goals to reach in an intriguing situation that operations are most exercised.
>
> (Piaget and Garcia 1971: 26, cited by Froebel Blockplay Research Group 1992: 75)

Block play and construction activities present children with opportunities to explore mathematical concepts. (It should be noted that the term 'blocks' is used in relation to materials which do not interlock, while the term bricks is more commonly used for those which do interlock, such as Lego.) While as we have seen 'any aspect of maths can crop up at any time' (Froebel Blockplay Research Group 1992: 91), blocks perhaps lend themselves to developing understanding of pattern and geometry (Froebel Blockplay Research Group 1992). The research group also points out that blocks appeal to both children's mathematical and aesthetic interests. They cite St Thomas Aquinas as suggesting that 'the senses delight in things duly proportioned' (Froebel Blockplay Research Group 1992: 89). Five-year-old Edward's response to his own block creation is described:

> 'I've done it! Fantastic!' He is radiant. Alessandros comes over to look: 'It's beautiful,' he says. 'I know,' says Edward. He prowls around and over his rectangular surface for several minutes, surveying his achievement and savouring its wholeness.

For confirmation of both the mathematical and aesthetic nature of blockplay you might take a look at a video on the QCDA website as guidance in completing the Early Years Foundation Stage profile (http://testsandexams.qcda.gov.uk/19391.aspx). Five-year-old Jaimin is building a pier and experiments with a beautiful arrangement of curved and triangular blocks to support the struts. Sadly the suggested profile entry highlights neither his considerable aesthetic abilities not his problem-solving strategies – perhaps another example of too narrow a view of what mathematics actually is.

Unit blocks are by their nature mathematical. Boaler (2009: 170) suggests that block building 'has been identified as one of the key reasons for success in mathematics all through school'. She goes on to indicate that, since boys generally play more with blocks than girls, it is likely to be the reason for boys' enhanced spatial abilities. The play and exploration gives them a sense of the internal logic which ensures that they fit together snugly and accurately and appeal to humans' 'mathematical minds'. Wood (1988: 199) describes the process of self-correction, an attribute essential to the development of a mathematical mind:

> The disposition to correct oneself is not an attribute of personality or ability. When children know, albeit intuitively, what *looks, sounds*, or *feels* right, we have reason to be confident that they will self-correct and self-instruct.

This, of course, implies that adults working with children also need to have an understanding of 'what *looks, sounds*, or *feels* right' and why. Blockplay often involves children in creating modules or routines. The Froebel Blockplay Research Group (1992: 80) suggest that 'in blockplay, a sign that a particular routine is well established occurs when children collect the exact shape, size and number of blocks required to carry it out. Sometimes they even preassemble subsections of a larger arrangement'.

The research group likens this ability to the subroutines involved in building more complex Logo programs and suggest that they may be used in developing understanding of 'primitives' or subroutines in programming. Blocks may also be used to heighten children's understanding of pattern. The mathematical relationships found between the blocks in a single set ensures that children can explore a number of options – identifying numerical and spatial patterns, and seeing the relationships between apparently different sized blocks.

Play with unit blocks provides mental mathematical models, a process which the Community Playthings website describes as 'absorbing' the concepts:

> The relationship between the 'unit' and the other block shapes creates an environment in which children develop motor skills and 'absorb' math concepts such as length, volume and fractions while totally engaged in the creative freedom of block play.
>
> (http://www.communityplaythings.co.uk)

The Froebel Blockplay Research Group suggests that blocks have a specific role to play in representing mathematical ideas:

> Links are forged enabling children to understand and make use of the relationships between mathematics embedded in practical situations and that represented in the disembodied symbolism of formal mathematics.
>
> The children have taught us that they will use both embedded and disembedded representations as appropriate to their present purposes in situations when it makes sense to them. Children (in the course of the project) have found their own important reasons to describe, draw and tally as part of their block play.
>
> (Gura 1992: 105)

The researchers in the Freobel Blockplay project often drew children's models. This became a habit copied by many children who began to record their own models in the same way. This is an excellent way to look at three-dimensional shapes anew, and can give an adult insight into how well children are perceiving shape. Moreover it gives children a new perspective on the shapes and relationships between them.

The development of block building

The following description of the stages of block building are to be found on Community Playthings website (http://www.community playthings.co.uk/resources/articles/block-building.html).

In Table 10.2, Gura (1992) defines the development of blockplay in terms of the frequency with which certain kinds of structures were made during the course of the research project. Stunt-building is frequently mentioned in this project. As children became familiar with particular kinds of building and the relationships between blocks they frequently attempted daring feats – representing ideas about the materials they were using. However, while interesting as part of the research, the ages indicated should not be taken as the only age group for which unit blocks are useful. Nor should it be taken as surprising if older children, who have not had such rich experiences, do not achieve comparable standards. As in so many matters, expertise comes with experience (Howe 1999, see Chapter 2).

Table 10.1 The stages of block building

Stage 1		Blocks are carried around but are not used for construction (usually very young children).
Stage 2	Building Begins	Children mostly make rows, either horizontal (on the floor) or vertical. There is much repetition in this early building pattern, which is basic functional play with blocks.
Stage 3	Bridging	Children create a bridge (or portal) by using two blocks to support a third. In architecture this is known as the post-and-lintel system
Stage 4	Enclosures	Children place blocks in such a way that they enclose a space. Bridging and enclosures are among the earliest technical problems children have to solve when playing with blocks, and they occur soon after a child begins to use blocks regularly.
Stage 5	Increasing use of imagination	With age, children become steadily more imaginative in their block building. They use more blocks and create more elaborate designs, incorporating patterns and balance into their constructions.
Stage 6	Named structures	Naming of structures for dramatic play begins. Before this stage, children may have named their structures, but not necessarily based on the function of the building. This stage of block building corresponds to the 'realistic' stage in art development.
Stage 7		Children use blocks to represent things they know, like cities, cars, airplanes, and houses. They also use blocks to stimulate dramatic play activities: zoo, farm, shopping center, and other locations.

Source: Based on Wardle (2002), citing Johnson. See http://www.communityplaythings.co.uk.

Table 10.2 The development of blockplay

Age	Frequency of types of block play	Frequent examples of figurative representations
3 and 4+	Some figurative building but focus on exploring • properties of blocks • combining them at increasing levels of integration and complexity • issues of space and movement	
3–5	2-and 3-dimensional patterns	
4+ – 5+	Equal amounts of time spent on exploring (as above) and figurative representations	1 Houses, buildings (sometimes named e.g. London Bridge) 2 Figures and furniture, transport and roads
6+	Focus on figurative representation	Groups of structures e.g. water, bridge and road

Source: Based on Gura (1992: 198–201).

Community Playthings also produce large wooden hollow blocks which are invaluable for creating large stable structures which children can climb safely on and which motivate collaborative play and activity. Although expensive, wooden materials of this sort last forever and this represent an excellent investment.

CONSTRUCTION SETS

Much of what been said about blocks applies to other types of construction sets – although many would dispute the idea that plastic materials can be compared to the aesthetic qualities of wood. In considering manipulatives in Chapter 5 of this book, some types of construction materials were mentioned. There is a huge range of types of construction sets – each offering different challenges, strengths and scales. As with blocks it is vital that there are sufficient of any one set to make construction meaningful for a group of children. Frustration and disaffection run high unless this is addressed.

An extremely interesting aspect of work with constructions sets is the work it opens up on robotics or gear ratios. A Lego set, for example, which can be used to make models which move in exciting and interesting ways, has a great deal of potential for developing not only information technology understanding but mathematical understanding related to time, sequence and so on too.

CREATIVE MATHEMATICS: BUILDING ON BUILDING

MakeBelieve Arts involved a group of children from Years 3 and 4 in considering the dilemmas facing town planners and cartographers.

MATHS FOCUS ***TOWN PLANNERS AND MAP MAKERS***

- Data handling
- Transforming two-dimensional materials into three dimensional

Scenario

A new town is going to be built, but before work can begin the town planners need to work out where all the buildings will be placed so that everything is in a convenient area. Once the town is built the mapmakers are called in, and it is their role to ensure that they keep a record of where everything is.

Exploration

1. A giant 8 square grid was marked out on the floor in tape. The children were then put into role as town planners and began to add houses, a school and shops on the various squares, thinking about where each of these should be in relation to each other.
2. Once all the pieces were placed children had the opportunity to review the town and see if any of the pieces needed to be moved or other buildings needed to be added.
3. When the town was completed the children mapped it out accurately onto a smaller grid.
4. Other pupils were then given an empty giant 8 square grid alongside the pieces that represented the buildings and the map of the town. They were invited to recreate the town using these items.

Outcomes

- This work was piloted with children from Year 3 and 4. The sophistication that they showed was greater than expected and the groups began to develop high quality maps to represent the town.

Quote from evaluation

I loved drawing my map after we had created the town. I wanted to make sure I got it exactly right so when we gave it to the other group they could build our town properly.

Year 4 pupil

TRANSFORMING THE TWO DIMENSIONAL TO THREE DIMENSIONAL

Two-dimensional work is a common feature of work on shape. Pattern blocks, which like wooden unit blocks are structured mathematically, provide insight into geometrical concepts. Four-year-old Marie was able to create a wide range of symmetrical shapes through informal play with them. She also become interested in finding out a number of different ways in which she could construct hexagons. This can be extended and made more exciting by for example working with pattern blocks and mirrors. If you add a mirror how many times is your model revealed? What if you add two or three mirrors? These materials can also engage older children who can devise games and activities which involve mathematical challenges and problems.

An aspect of mathematical construction which we have not yet considered is the processes by which something two-dimensional (such as a piece of paper) can be turned into a three-dimensional object (such as a box or a model). Children can find this process enchanting, containing as it does an element of magic. Indeed adults can too. Recent newspaper articles featured the work of a Canadian architecture student. Mui-Ling Teh has produced tiny origami models, some as small as 3millimetres (see http://www.telegraph.co.uk/news/picturegalleries/howaboutthat/7166758/Tiny-origami-models-created-by-Mui-Ling-Teh.html). For many years origami was seen as something for children – just following the instructions in the Rupert Annual. More recently however it has been recognised as an exciting branch of mathematics – undertaken by real mathematicians (see for example Alperin 2000; and Demaine and O'Rourke 2008) for real purposes (see for example Newton 2009).

Devlin (2000: 259–60) argues that what we actually need to teach children about mathematics is not simply about getting the right mathematical answer but should:

> design courses that demonstrate what mathematics and science are and what role they play in modern life, rather than teach particular skills. These courses would more closely resemble typical history or social skills courses than existing mathematics and science courses. Their arithmetical and manipulative-algebraic content 'problem solving' work would be included to give a feel for what is involved, and the goal would be completion of the task, not a 'perfect performance' or 'getting the right answer'.

This, he suggests, would meet the traditional goal of education since it would ensure that human culture was passed on – rather than simply vocational or functional training. If we link this to another of Devlin's premises (and indeed one that is central to this book) that narrative (or gossip as he provocatively terms it) is central to learning, then it begins to make perfect sense. Of course teachers can do both – ensuring that children are familiar with the narratives of mathematics and the development of mathematical understanding are not mutually exclusive. If intrigue and interest are what make us want to know more, then origami has much to offer.

Origami is the branch of mathematics that has supported the development of robotics (Kanade 1980; Demaine and O'Rourke 2008). It is the branch of mathematics which made the Hubble Telescope possible (http://californiaconnected.org/tv/archives/147). Imagine the excitement engendered by explaining to children that in order to construct a telescope light and compact enough to be sent into space, yet strong enough to be of value, scientists made use of origami techniques.

In folding models, there are many examples of places where words like square, triangle, parallelogram, trapezium, isosceles, scalene, obtuse-angled, triangle, pentagon, hexagon etc can be used in a perfectly natural way. Fractions and angles are an integral part of the folding process. The transformation of square to triangles, triangles to trapeziums and so on gives a new perspective on the world of shape. In addition they underpin the transformation from two-dimensional to three-dimensional which becomes apparent as the model emerges.

Another activity involving 2- to 3-D transformation is the more traditionally included work on nets. Simply by collecting and storing boxes as flat nets rather than three-dimensional shapes, children are presented with a puzzle. This can be done with small boxes for junk modelling or design technology purposes or with large boxes for building outdoors or in a larger space such as a hall. Two books on skyscrapers and bridges (full details shown at the end of the chapter) might offer a starting point for children who may lack creative confidence.

Upitis *et al.* (1997) describe a jewellery making activity undertaken with 8- and 9-year-olds. Rena Upitis describes her long-held interest in making paper jewels – which she claims began in childhood when a teacher reprimanded her for absent-mindedly wrapping a strip of paper around her pencil. When challenged she claimed she was making jewellery. She describes the process which she finds so exciting:

> We invited (the children) to cut various shapes from the paper, and then to roll the paper or in some other way turn it into a three-dimensional object from the flat two-dimensional piece of paper. I am particularly fond of the effect that comes from rolling a long right angled triangle, and I demonstrated this effect to the class.
>
> (Upitis *et al.* 1997: 81)

A description of the children's experimentation follows – involving scalene, isosceles and right-angled triangles, of different sizes and papers. The way in which the children sort through a collection of beads is described as 'purposeful', different from the early sorting that goes on in classrooms in that:

> in order to make the kind of jewellery you have in mind, you sometimes have to sort along a number of different dimensions or attributes before the right beads are found . . . Some people never stop sorting and classifying – after all, biologists spend their lifetimes sorting and describing independent and overlapping sets of objects . . . [A] prominent computer scientist. . . . speculates there are enough new problems in biology alone to keep scholars occupied for the next 500 years.
>
> (Upitis *et al.* 1997: 83)

The gender aspects of this task are discussed. The class teacher was worried that boys might not be motivated but reflects that she often introduces activities which are chosen with boys in mind. Despite some initial reticence from some boys they all engage enthusiastically – but when they see that one boy is making a Star Trek communicator badge, interest levels soar. The class teacher comments on the way in which transforming two-dimensional materials into three-dimensional objects changes her own way of seeing:

> Now I looked at shapes – both finished shapes, and shapes that I imagined were there initially, in two dimensions. This reminded me of my experience with tessellations, when previously unobserved maths started popping out at me from

unexpected places. With jewellery, I looked at size changes and thought about scale transformations: I looked at shapes and thought about geometric combinations, and I looked at pleasing designs and thought of symmetry and balance.

Finally, consider the design technology tasks which can be undertaken with rolled up newspaper. Students constructed a giant tetrahedron using rolled up newspapers – in much the same way as Construct-o-straws might be used.

CONCLUDING THOUGHTS

Play with two- and three-dimensional shapes appears to give the human mind new ways of seeing and understanding them. Transformations are involved in:

- changing something two dimensional into a three-dimensional shape
- creating two-dimensional representations of three-dimensional constructions
- building, deconstructing, modifying and reconstructing structures from blocks or other construction materials
- creating moving objects from stationary materials.

Transformation, translation or transduction are vital aspects of creativity. The power and engaging powers of these particular processes should not be overlooked since not only are they creative but they are also mathematical.

FURTHER READING

Gura, P. (1992) *Exploring Learning: Young Children and Blockplay*. London: Paul Chapman Publishing.

Upitis, R., Phillips, E. and Higginson, W. (1997) *Creative Mathematics*. London: Routledge (see Chapter 4).

The following websites offer free instructions for a range of origami projects:
http://www.origami-resource-center.com
http://www.mathsyear2000.org/explorer/origami/2-waytube/

CHILDREN'S BOOKS

Clements, G. (2007) *A Picture History of Great Buildings*. London: Frances Lincoln Children's Books.

Hutchins, P. (1987) *Changes, Changes*. New York: Aladdin Paperbacks.

Jam, S. (2005) *The Paper Princess*. Hong Kong: PPP Ltd.

This is the story of 'the world's greatest folder upper'. Quirky but entertaining and containing some truths about paper folding.

Johmann, C. and Rieth, E. (1999) *Bridges: Amazing Structures to Design, Build and Test*. Charlotte, Vermont: Williamson Publishing Company.

Johmann, C. and Rieth, E. (2001) *Skyscrapers: Amazing Structures to Design, Build and Test*. Charlotte, Vermont: Williamson Publishing Company.

Jones, R. (2009) *See Inside Famous Buildings*. London: Usborne.

Roeder, A. (2009) *13 Buildings Children Should Know*. London: Prestel.

Thorne-Thomsen, K. (1994) *Frank Lloyd Wright for Kids*. Chicago; Chicago Review Press.

CHAPTER 11

EXPLORING MATHEMATICS THROUGH MUSIC

There is a strongly held popular belief that music and mathematics are inextricably linked. Marcus du Sautoy (2004: 77) asserts that there is a natural link, adding that 'Mathematics departments invariably have little trouble assembling an orchestra from the ranks of their members'. The link is sometimes made in teaching music – especially if students are being taught primarily through the use of notations. They may be asked to do the sums involved in calculating rests, dotted notes and hemi-demi-semi quavers. However, music is rarely used as a tool for teaching mathematics. A notable exception may be that in the early years number rhymes are used to teach children to count. This reflects an implicit understanding of the role that music plays in supporting memory.

However, music has much more to offer mathematics than simply a role as a mnemonic. It is thought by many (see for example Egan 1991; du Sautoy 2004; Brandt 2009) to have been the biological and cultural starting point for the development of mathematical thinking in humans. Rhythms emerge or develop in human activity and support those activities. You have only to think of a group of people, without the benefits of machinery, moving heavy loads, to think of the advantage which rhythmic movement offers (Egan 1991). Some writers suggest that numbers arose from our fingers while others prefer to link the origins of counting to dance (Brandt 2009). Whatever the case, theorists from many disciplines are clear about the role that music played in bringing rhythm and thus an understanding of time to human consciousness. Leibniz, a seventeenth-century German polymath, reflected this idea from a different perspective, writing that 'Music is the pleasure the human mind experiences from counting without being aware that it is counting' (cited by du Sautoy 2004: 77–8).

Perhaps the most obvious way in which music and mathematics interrelate lies in the physics of sound. In simple terms the length of a vibrating string or column of air determines the pitch it plays. Children can be invited to compare, say, the sound of a small drum or xylophone with the sound of a large instrument of the same type. The general rule is that larger instruments or objects make lower sounds, although you should always be aware that there are exceptions to this.

The relationship between sound and pitch is one which has fascinated mathematicians for thousands of years (du Sautoy 2004) and one which can continue to engage children. Pitch was perhaps the main interest of Pythagoras (Harkleroad 2006) – which is probably surprising since he is more readily linked to geometry in the popular mind. Harkleroad (2006) also writes of the position of music in the middle ages when music was linked to arithmetic, geometry and astronomy as the paths to knowledge. For children, the use of Boomwhackers can illustrate the relationship between size and pitch very well.

Junk materials can also be used to demonstrate this principle. By taking plastic tubing (such as that used for drainpipes) and cutting it into different lengths (with an ordinary small hacksaw), you can produce the notes of a familiar do-re-mi (major) scale. The tubes can be made to sound by holding them lightly and hitting them on the end with a ruler or small bat (like a small table tennis bat). They can also be mounted on a frame and used outdoors. If you are interested in producing a major scale of 8 notes, the following measurements will work:

120 cm; 108 cm; 96 cm; 90 cm; 80 cm; 72 cm; 64 cm; 60cm

While music has its own intrinsic value and worth and should not be seen as simply a tool for learning and teaching other subjects, it can offer creative, exciting and challenging ways to develop students' mathematical understanding. The role of music in promoting the playfulness associated with creative thinking and learning has been well documented (Bresler 2004; Malloch and Trevarthen 2009). On a more solemn note the aesthetics of mathematics has led to it being referred to, like music, as 'a creative art' in which ideas should fit together 'harmoniously' (du Sautoy 2004: 78, citing Hardy). Harkleroad (2006: 1) draws attention to the way in which both music and mathematics:

> combine the intellectual and the aesthetic in a wonderful blend. Unfortunately nonmusicians often remain unaware of the rich intellectual content of music, and nonmathematicians likewise of the equally rich aesthetic side of math.

CREATIVE TEACHING

For teachers wishing to teach creatively and to awaken creative learning in children, music offers many exciting opportunities. It is clear that music and mathematics have a number of fundamental, or perhaps elemental, links. Harkleroad (2006: 1) suggests that 'abstract patterns form the stock-in-trade of each' and that in order 'to express these patterns, each has developed its own symbolic language'. Learning about one approach to pattern and the symbols with which it can be represented not merely supports but enhances learning in the other (Egan 1991).

Exploring mathematics through music is highly motivating for children, as indicated in the Cambridge Primary Review (Alexander 2010). Music takes up a very high proportion of everyone's time at least outside of school. Sadly it takes up relatively small amounts of time in school! But in the real world as Hargreaves (2004) points out an average of 40 per cent of our waking lives is spent listening to music. In fact, this would be a great mathematical investigation – working out the average listening times for different age groups, families, classes and so on.

In addition, music is said to support the development of a number of personal qualities (Music Education Council submission to the Cambridge Primary Review, in Alexander 2010) many of which can contribute to mathematical understanding. These might include the development of language; concentration, and self-discipline. Hallam (2001) has investigated claims that music has an impact on cognitive understanding and draws a number of conclusions – two of which are pertinent here. She writes:

> Taking music was positively related to better performance in other subjects, [but] this does not necessarily mean that it was the cause of it . . . From our current level of knowledge it is not possible to draw firm conclusions about the effects of listening or active involvement in music making on our intellectual skills. The jury remains out.
>
> (Hallam 2001: 15–16)

She does however concede that musical activity 'appears to have a significant positive effect on the development of characteristics of creativity' (2001: 58). It is clear that music and mathematics have many links. In the sections that follow, some ways in which these links can be developed and extended creatively in order to support mathematical understanding are given.

MEMORY FOR MATHEMATICAL FACTS

One of the universal features of music is that it is used to support memory (Pound and Harrison 2003). Advertising jingles and alphabet songs underline this function in our everyday lives. In schools and other early childhood settings, number rhymes are used to help children remember number names in the correct order and if these are accompanied by finger actions they are an even more powerful aid to memory. This is because the part of the brain responsible for numbers is adjacent to the part of the brain responsible for fingers (Ramachandran and Blakeslee 1999). Every teacher of young children has a ready store of counting songs, many with accompanying finger actions.

The musical elements used do not have to be fully worked out tunes – rhythmic chanting and movement will also support memory. Egan (1991) reminds us that while in literate societies written language or symbols are a key means of supporting thought, in aliterate cultures, people use a number of different tools for thinking. These include music, dance and poetry – as well as narrative. As we have seen, children's attempts to learn mathematics are akin to those of someone learning a new language (Worthington and Carruthers 2006; Boaler 2009). In order to be able to use mathematics at more than a barely functional level, children need to become fluent users of mathematical language. Just as songs are used to support the development of bilingualism, so they can be used to support children in becoming bi-numerate, fluent users of mathematical language and thinking. Songs and rhymes which employ mathematical language give children a ready bank of relevant words and phrases.

Books such as *Tom Thumb's Musical Maths* (MacGregor 1998) include a range of songs, written to fit in with well-known tunes, which explore some other aspects of mathematics, rather than simply counting. There are songs about shape, songs about adding and multiplying. Other existing commercial materials (see for example resources available from http://www.beam.co.uk or http://www.songsforteaching.com/mathsongs.htm) can also be used. However, the beauty of this approach is that it can encourage adults and children alike to make up their own songs and rhymes to reinforce the learning of mathematical facts. The simplest way is to use a known tune – preferably one which repeats phrases and does not require a rhyme. Tunes which lend themselves well to this idea are *London Bridge is Falling Down*, *Here we go round the Mulberry Bush, Polly put the Kettle on* and so on. Below is an example of children creating raps to help them remember a range of facts. These of course do not need a tune.

Raps are popular and make things memorable for children. In this example, children were invited to create a number of raps to help them memorise crucial facts. This was written by five Year 6 pupils who were struggling with remembering the difference between mode, mean and median.

You've got 2, 4, 4 and 8.
Find the mean before it's too late.
We add them together and divide by 4
Cos that's how many numbers we have to explore.
Mean – Mean – The average machine!

You've got 2, 4, 4 and 8.
Find the mode before it's too late.
Mode is the one that comes round more.
In this case it's gonna be 4.
Mode – Mode – The popular code!

You've got 2, 4, 4 and 8.
Find the median before it's too late.
Put them in order, find the middle.
That's the answer to the median riddle.
Median – Median – The middle's the median!

Here is a rhyme created by another group from the same class to remind them about lines:

Ver-tic-al,
stand up straight and touch the sky
If you're tired be horizontal,
lie down, touch the ground
Diagonal lines up against the wall
But vertical stand straight up tall

Ver-ti-cal is straight
that's right mate, straight,

Chorus:

We're talking lines of different kinds
We're talking lines
With different rhymes
We're talking lines so don't forget it
Because if you do you will regret it
(if you do you will regret it)

Parallel lines never meet
Look to the horizon for the horizontal beat
Vertex like a mountain top
Perpendicular. 90 degrees then stop
Bisect means to cut a line in half
A bendy line is called an arc.

This rhyme was accompanied by hand movements that children could be seen demonstrating silently to themselves in a subsequent test. (Some mathematicians argue that parallel lines may meet at infinity but this is something of a philosophical debate. The teacher, in this instance – and just before SATs – was content to take the general definition such as this simple one 'parallel lines will never meet, no matter how far they are extended' (http://www.mathsisfun.com/geometry/parallel-lines.html)).

It is also possible to use a call and response technique to get children to create and remember the words to a new memory song. The teacher chants the first line and in groups or pairs the children have to write a second line as a response to call back. By asking the children themselves to come up with responses we generate an ownership of the piece rather than it being something that someone else has written for them to learn.

RHYTHM AND TIME

Rhythmic vocalisations often link with rhythmic movement. Many writers looking back at human history present a link between rhythmic movement and the development of mathematical thinking (see, for example, Brandt 2009 and Mithen 2005). If music and dance are considered as internalised counting, there are many creative musical activities which can be used to promote mathematical understanding. *Let's Go Shoolie-Shoo* (MacGregor and Gargreave 2004) and *Let's Go Zudie-o* (MacGregor and Gargreave 2001) include many examples of music in which the rhythm can readily be felt. Many British folk tunes have this quality, which is why folk dancing can be attractive to all ages. Group dancing offers an opportunity to develop the internalised counting of those who appear to have difficulty in holding a rhythm.

The mirror neurons in the brain encourage imitation – in fact the brain itself mirrors or imitates the brain of others engaged in physical actions (Rizzolatti and Craighero, 2005). A book like *Tanka Tanka Skunk* (Webb 2003) encourages rhythmic chanting and is very much enjoyed (and emulated) by young children. The example below was actually a Year 7 project but demonstrates the kinds of learning which can be explored through musical activity. The physical action reinforces the learning, offering another 'way of knowing' (Claxton 1997).

Children often enjoy listening to Steve Reich's piece *Clapping Music* – perhaps not least because it challenges their ideas about what music is. The piece was written

MATHS FOCUS ***MUSIC FRACTIONS***

- Fractions

Exploration

1 We demonstrate the component parts of bars of music with four different groups of children by clapping different beats of the bar.
   - Group 1 clapping once every count of 4 to represent the whole beat
   - Group 2 clapping twice every count of 4 on the count of 1 and 3
   - Group 3 clapping quarter beats on every count
   - Group 4 clapping eighth beats – 1 and 2 and 3 and 4 and
2 We then invited four children to stand between two canes to form a visual representation of one bar of music. We asked them to take turns to clap one beat to represent where they stood in the bar. So the first child clapped, then the second etc.
3 Next the children were asked to separate the bar in half so that we just hear the first half of it (i.e. only the first two children clapping).
4 Then we listened to three quarters of the bar and finally one quarter.
5 We extended the activity to include 6/ 8/ 12 and 16 children in the bar. Each time we looked at breaking the bar down into differing fractions.

Outcomes

- Some of the Year 6 pupils struggled with this initially, but surprisingly a number of children who normally struggle with fractions really began to grasp it. For children who have strong musical intelligence this type of approach can reach them where other methods might not.
- Some of the children who were normally very good at maths found this way difficult, and it began to build an understanding between the whole class of how it feels when you find something difficult, especially as they could see children who normally struggled excelling in this lesson.

Quote from evaluation

Music was really fun. It was like you could learn stuff by clapping and rapping. I remember clapping the beats and seeing how much can go into a number which helped me. It was fun, like I could do anything. I felt like I was really good, normally I am rubbish at maths and get told off a lot.

Year 6 pupil

for two performers. One claps a basic rhythm in 12/8 time, throughout the piece. The other claps the same pattern, but regularly adjusts the pattern moving it away from the basic or initial rhythm one beat at a time. Eventually, after 144 bars the two performers are once again playing in unison.

DEVELOPING UNDERSTANDING OF PATTERN

If mathematics is the 'science of pattern' (Devlin 2000), music and dance are undoubtedly the 'art of pattern'. Pattern and structure are inherent to both areas of discipline – the art and the science. The human brain enjoys pattern, both seeking it out and creating it (Lucas 2001). Devlin (2000) suggests that it is this characteristic which led us to develop mathematics. As we noted in Chapter 1, the DCSF recognise pattern as one of five major aspects of what mathematics is – both in number and shape (National Strategies 2006). This makes it even more surprising that a document entitled *Numbers and Patterns: Laying Foundations in Mathematics* (National Strategies 2009b) makes no attempt to define pattern.

Although pattern is such a strong part of human thinking and activity, many children and adults find it surprisingly difficult to describe pattern – to identify the characteristics. Zebra skin, for example, is not regular or symmetrical but it is a pattern because it is identifiable as such. Although, as has been reiterated in this book, we are born pattern seekers, mathematical patterns remain a complex issue for many children – and as such some children may need help in understanding it. Describing patterns found in the environment, in pictures, fabrics, events and so on can help by giving children some of the relevant vocabulary – such as sequential, repeating, symmetrical, growing, increasing, decreasing, alternating, cyclical, radial and staircase patterns (Pound 2008). Representing the same patterns aurally and visually is another way to explore the concepts involved.

A group of children made up aural patterns – some used body percussion, some used voice and some used instruments and other sound-makers. Each group played their pattern and then tried to represent it visually – using a range of natural and structural materials. So a group of children had created a cyclical pattern using first one, then two, then three sounds – until they reached six sounds and then returned to one. Initially the sounds used were simply claps. Since there were five in the group, and the clapping continued for several rounds, each time a child had another turn they had to clap a different number of times.

```
                    X                       X
                X   X                   X   X
            X   X   X               X   X   X
        X   X   X   X           X   X   X   X
    X   X   X   X   X       X   X   X   X   X       X
X   X   X   X   X   X   X   X   X   X   X   X   X   X
1   2   3   4   5   1   2   3   4   5   1   2   3   4
```

(1–5 identifies children in the group taking their turn; x indicates the number of sounds made by each child.)

They represented this pattern by setting out rows of buttons in a circle – rather like rays of the sun. They then tried creating the pattern – each using a different sound. This time they represented the pattern with shells – using six different kinds of shells to represent the six sounds. They also experimented with using a range of other materials – twigs and pebbles; pattern blocks and unifix. Of particular interest was the discussion which surrounded the decisions of this and other groups – about whether the representation should be read horizontally or vertically, which material or resource would best represent the sounds made and so on.

ENJOYING MATHEMATICS CREATIVELY

In addition to the opportunities for exploring mathematical ideas creatively which have been outlined in this chapter, it would be a pity not to acknowledge the role of music and dance in allowing children to think while lessening the constraints usually placed on them. In focusing on music and the physical movement which, in children, invariably accompanies it, we give them opportunities to shift to the more creative, unconscious thinking which promotes creative thought. In everyday language, it helps them to lighten up and think outside the box. The mathematical understanding that emerges from these experiences feels very different from the mathematical thinking that comes about through discussion or through paper and pencil work. But that does not make it less valuable – it simply means that adults are helping children to tap into a variety of 'ways of knowing'. These, in turn, reinforce one another.

Work which may be loosely described as creative is often linked to learning styles. Eminent psychologists working in different fields Greenfield, Claxton and Gardner are agreed (see Pound 2009) that a focus on learning styles will not support this rich learning. What they are agreed upon is that the workings of the brain benefit most from sensory input on all channels – in short the importance of using a variety of media goes way beyond any learning preferences. All learning and learners benefit from a wide range of sensory input. Music is often marginalised – yet it is one of the few disciplines which relies on both temporal and spatial awareness. It is this which has led Odam (1995: 19) to describe music and dance as 'a unique schooling for the brain'.

Finally we cannot leave this chapter without drawing attention to the fact that a musical performance will of itself provide a range of opportunities for thinking mathematically. The work of Upitis *et al.* (1997) on animation, which was outlined in Chapter 8, included music. Wyse and Dowson (2009) highlight the creativity involved in producing a musical or mini-opera. The music is clear but the mathematical thinking involved is perhaps less obvious. Nonetheless creating and playing music (possibly including the use of ICT); devising and performing dances; planning and scheduling the event; and problem solving throughout the process can all, as we have seen, contribute to a creative approach to mathematics.

FURTHER READING

Brandt, P. A. (2009) 'Music and how we became human: a view from cognitive semiotics', in S. Malloch and C. Trevarthen (eds) *Communicative Musicality*. Oxford: Oxford University Press.

Devlin, K. (2000) *The Maths Gene*. London: Weidenfeld and Nicolson (see section on pattern).
du Sautoy, M. (2004) *The Music of the Primes*. London: Harper Perennial.
Harkleroad, L. (2006) *The Math behind the Music*. New York: Cambridge University Press.

CHILDREN'S BOOKS

Webb, S. (2003) *Tanka Tanka Skunk*. London:Random House.

CHAPTER 12

CONCLUSION: LEARNING MATHEMATICS THROUGH PLAYFUL TEACHING

The focus throughout this book has been on four types of creativity – creative teaching, creative learning, creative partnerships and creative mathematics. These four aspects work together to produce an approach which may be called teaching for creativity. All rely on a creative and therefore playful teacher – someone prepared to take risks; entertain new ideas; and with a sense of wonder and curiosity about the world around them. Time and time again in researching for this book, it has become apparent that the chosen approach is only as good as the teacher – in using, for example, manipulatives or apparatus, or in exploring origami, and in a general willingness to be playful, curious, adventurous and enthusiastic. The teacher in the example that follows was playful, willing to take risks, and demonstrated both a sense of fun and trust in the children.

The flexibility of thinking involved in playfulness is the essence of creativity. As with all other aspects of teaching, teaching mathematics creatively requires a number of characteristics and skills. In this chapter we will attempt to draw these elements together.

TEACHING FOR CREATIVITY

QCDA's website (http://curriculum.qcda.gov.uk/key-strategies-1-and-2/learning-across-the-curriculum/creativity/howcanteacherspromotecreativity/index.aspx) suggests that teachers can promote creativity by:

- *Actively encourag(ing) pupils to question, make connections, envisage what might be and explore ideas. Promote and reward imagination and originality.* Curiosity, making unusual connections and the use of imagination support creativity. However as we have shown, they are also vital elements of mathematical understanding. All three enable children to find problems and

MEMORISING FACTS

Imagine sitting in a hall with a group of Year 6 pupils prior to SATs and apparently wasting time that could be spent on serious revision for an afternoon creating stories, riddles and rhymes. What are the number properties that we need to remember and how can we make remembering them a joyful experience for our pupils? Rather than testing the knowledge that they already have, we can try giving out the formulas with the task of creating a way to remember these using a range of learning approaches that will appeal to the whole class.

Prime numbers can be remembered by dividing them up between the class and so that in groups of 4–5 they each get 3–4 numbers. The task is for each group to come up with a short story or phrase around their numbers that they can recite as a group accompanied by actions. As each group creates their number stories and actions they need to ensure they develop something that they can teach to the rest of the class. For example:

2 elephants ate 3 currant buns and then slept for 5 minutes.
7 dwarfs climbed onto the number 11 bus which was filled with 13 witches.

Once each group has created their rhymes or mnemonic they teach each other the lines and actions. As the teaching continues pupils are questioned to further embed the numbers in their memory. How many witches, how many current buns, how long did the elephants sleep for?

Imagine an afternoon revising prime numbers spent asking questions like how many dwarfs climbed onto the bus and how many elephants were there? Surely this is much more playful than asking pupils to name three prime numbers? (See also p. 73 for additional examples.)

maintain the enthusiasm needed to be a successful mathematician. Curiosity, wanting to know is vital to both problem-solving and the perseverance needed to see a problem through to a satisfactory outcome. Making unusual connections supports analysis of data while imagination enables children to make representations or tools for thinking about mathematics.

Asking children to explain their reasoning makes it possible to promote unusual thinking. It may take time for children to explain and they may need support to do it. If we are to help children to be mathematically creative adults must also demonstrate mathematical creativity. Children may present ideas which we have not considered before and we must be willing to listen and explore. As we noted in Chapter 1, creativity may sometimes be a mixed blessing!

- *Ask(ing) open-ended questions such as 'What if. . .?' and 'How might you. . .?' to help pupils see things from different perspectives.*

In order to promote creative thinking in general adults should avoid asking closed questions. Mathematics is an area of the curriculum in which it is all too easy to drift into wanting one single correct answer. This approach is an anathema to creativity. Williams (1996) suggests that responding to apparently correct answers and those displaying apparent misconceptions in the same way will help. Simply asking children to explain how they arrived at an answer will provoke an open-ended response – rather than a teacher-pleasing pat answer. It is not always easy to find the questions which will challenge children to think in creative ways but the more adults try to do this, the more children will pick up on those ideas challenge one another and themselves. Adults also need to be mindful of research (see for example Walsh and Sattes 2005) that highlights the way in which we fail to give children sufficient thinking time. Most adults rush in with another question before the first one is answered.

- *Valu(ing) and prais(ing) what pupils do and say. Establish an atmosphere in which they feel safe to say things, take risks and respond creatively.*

  Praise needs to be specific. Simply saying 'great!' or 'fantastic!' doesn't allow children to pinpoint what you are praising and why. 'Well done for not giving up, but sticking with it even when it went wrong!' or 'I really like the way you have tessellated those shapes – how do you think the pattern might be extended' is much more likely to enable children to repeat and build on their success.

  Risk-taking is an essential element of creativity. Mathematics is an area of the curriculum where most people, children and adults alike, lack confidence and therefore find it hard to take risks. A shift to a more conjectural, more problem-solving approach will support improved confidence.

- *Creat(ing) a fun, relaxed working environment if you want to encourage pupils to be adventurous and explore ideas freely.*

  Drama, role play, story, outdoor experiences, music and dance are all likely to be perceived by children as fun. The notion of *hard fun* which was described in Chapter 3 should be the aim of creative mathematics. In order to be adventurous, children need to be challenged – they have to want to find out in order to engage with a task.

- *Creat(ing) conditions for quiet reflection and concentration if you want to encourage pupils to work imaginatively.*

  Organising the classroom, indoors and out, in such a way as to both support collaborative work and play and promote quiet, reflective and focused activity is a challenge. How this is achieved will be depend on the space available and the ethos of the school. The rate of change towards this goal will also depend on a whole school approach. As noted earlier, parents and staff often have to shift their perceptions of what mathematics is and how creativity can possibly be applied to it before progress can be made. Claxton (2008) reminds us that children need unhurried time if they are to reflect and think flexibly. When children are urged to rush, when pace becomes more important than thinking, we tend to revert to well-rehearsed modes of thinking rather than the 'out of the box' thinking required for creativity (Claxton 1997).

- *Mak(ing) the most of unexpected events. When appropriate, put aside your lesson plan and 'go with the moment', but never lose sight of your overall learning objectives.*

- *Be(ing) willing to stand back and let pupils take the lead. However, make sure that you are always on hand to provide prompts and support as needed.*

  Most learning objectives can be achieved in a number of different ways. The fact that children's interests shift to take in something new or novel need not be a problem. Evaluation of the day's teaching will inform decisions about whether the unexpected event served the planned learning objectives, whether they need to be addressed in a new way, and what other learning objectives may have been met.

Where children take the initiative, this is not a cue to busy yourself with something else. To ensure that it is a learning experience it is essential that you tune into what is happening. You don't have to talk, or suggest – sometimes you can just wait and see – which is not always easy for teachers.

- *Join(ing) in with activities and model creative thinking and behaviour. Showing the pupils that you are a learner too can help to create an open, constructive learning environment.*
  Mathematics is an area of the curriculum where many members of staff are not sufficiently confident to admit to not knowing something but being a learner is an essential element of creativity. Creativity emerges from new thinking and from challenging our own existing thinking. Showing children that we are prepared to do that will help them to feel safe enough to take the risks necessary for creative mathematical thinking and learning.
- *Giv(ing) pupils opportunities to work with others from their class, year group and different age groups.*
  There is strong evidence that explaining things to others helps us to understand (see Chapter 3; Lee 2006; Mercer and Littleton 2007). Cross-phase work, like that described in Chapter 7, is powerful and rewarding. Older children working with younger, children with additional learning needs finding a valuable niche; those whose spoken or written English is not well developed exploring mathematics through drama or painting; those who are good at spoken or written English being challenged to think through a different and perhaps less comfortable medium – all of these things are possible and manageable. They involve some creative risk-taking of both adults and children but they can produce exciting and memorable mathematics.

CREATIVE MATHEMATICS

Teaching mathematics creatively involves rethinking the nature of mathematics held by many – including teachers, parents and support staff. It involves reconceptualising what mathematics is – entailing problem solving and pattern and with a focus on the application across the curriculum. It will involve going way beyond numbers; beyond the purely instrumental or functional aspects of mathematics, beyond the mere entitlement to demonstrate to children the excitement and the beauty of mathematics. And perhaps above all, it will go beyond 'curriculum delivery'. We should remember Paley's phrase (1981) that children are often only in 'temporary custody' of mathematical ideas and concepts – until something has been learnt we haven't taught it. We will need to revisit, re-present and make mathematics memorable, by making it creative.

Mathematics is much more than numeracy and, as we explored in Chapter 1, it is in the beauty of mathematics that some children and adults become enthusiastic (see for example du Sautoy 2008). By encouraging children to explore mathematics in their own way, we help them to find both the creative beauty and the creative energy that will support learning. This will mean harnessing the imagination which is at the heart of human endeavour (Ramachandran 2004).

CREATIVE PARTNERSHIPS

Throughout this book the immense value of learning to work together in order to foster creative mathematics has been reiterated. Collaboration amongst children is vital but the partnerships do not stop there. We need to create communities of learners – parents and staff working together. This is essential if children are to come to understandings about the true nature of mathematics. Only in this way can the creative approach to mathematics which will fit children for their adult life in our ever-changing world be realised. We need to draw in the community and we need to undertake the additional training proposed for primary mathematics specialists. But being the specialist does not mean having all the answers.

There will need to be a partnership between members of staff. All phase specialists as well as subject specialists can work together to reach consensus on the kinds of integrated approaches which will bring mathematics to life. Cross-phase work draws children and staff together, developing the sense of progress in learning and a sense of a learning community. Co-operation is also needed between staff to ensure that art and mathematics or history and mathematics learning in both subjects is enhanced and one is not compromising the integrity of the other.

The conventional sense of creative partnerships – of working with creative artists is also important. Although relatively rare, MakeBelieve Arts, for example, has been able to take on creative partnership work in schools, focusing on the development of mathematical understanding. This gives recognition and status to the role that the creative arts, and in this case drama in particular, can play in making mathematics more real for children.

Much lip service is paid to the idea of partnership with parents but it is not always easy to achieve. Although frequently described as partners, parents are rarely thought of as creative partners. In fact, as Boaler (2009) points out, parents have a vital role to play in helping children to become creative mathematicians. She devotes a whole chapter to the early beginnings of mathematical thinking and on the role that parents play in its development. The problem for schools is that attitudes (in children and parents) have already hardened by the time children arrive at school. One London borough has produced a booklet for the parents of young children. Entitled *More to Maths than Counting* (Tower Hamlets 2009) it offers suggestions of activities which are fun and a simple part of everyday life to support children's interest and enthusiasm for mathematics.

By far the most important aspect of a creative partnership needs to be with children. Teachers and support staff need to tune into children's thinking. Clark (2005) describes the careful observation and intent listening to them as 'ways of seeing' – giving an enhanced understanding of their thinking. Teachers frequently claim to start where the child is, but unless we really listen to what their words and actions tell us about their mathematical understanding and their motivations and interests, we will be unable to determine where that is.

Creative partnerships between pupils are also productive. Cross-phase work can be very liberating – younger children are motivated by proximity to older ones; older children learn what they know (and don't know) by beginning to articulate it in a new way; less able children have a chance to shine – while as we saw in the previous chapter, the competence of the more able can be questioned and extended by having to think in new ways. A focus on measurement (Wyse and Dowson 2009: 43) would be a great cross-phase topic or project. They suggest, for example, a check that all classes have the right size chairs for the relevant children. This would be followed up by strategies to improve provision. It is also suggested that children's horizons on measurement could be extended by measuring noise and light levels. A focus of this nature could involve every child in the school – with real purpose and an opportunity to learn from and with others.

CREATIVE LEARNERS

According to an Ofsted report, creative learning emerges when children are encouraged to question, to make connections and to see relationships. It is also based on an ability to speculate, to pursue a line of enquiry flexibly, and to reflect and review critically (Ofsted 2010). In order to develop the children we work with as creative learners we should be trying to nurture a range of characteristics. We want active learners – physically and mentally. We want confident learners, prepared to take intellectual risks, capable of enjoying the challenge of hard fun. In order to be creative, children will need to be encouraged to make unusual connections. They know how to do it – but a curriculum which focuses on one right answer will quickly discourage them from making anything but safe, tried and tested connections. Unusual connections are evident in humorous interludes and will be supported where children are able to engage in dialogues and negotiation both with peers and adults.

Creative learners make use of opportunities to exercise their curiosity and enthusiasm, seek challenges and be intrigued by the world around them. They will make full use of their imagination and enjoy the conjectural thinking which means they will strive to look for alternatives and developments. Creative learners emerge when teaching is 'dialogic'. Mercer and Littleton (2007: 42) define dialogic teaching as:

1. [giving children] . . . opportunities and encouragement to question, state points of view, and comment on ideas and issues that arise in lessons;
2. the teacher engages in discussion with students which explore and support the development of their understanding of content;
3. the teacher takes students' contributions into account in developing the subject theme of the lesson and in devising activities that enable students to pursue their understanding themselves, through talk and other activity;
4. the teacher uses talk to provide a cumulative, continuing, contextual frame to enable students' involvement with the new knowledge they are encountering.

Children also emerge as creative learners when they are supported in becoming collaborative learners. Investigations work well for this, particularly if they involve physical action. An activity such as this one (suggested by Wyse and Dowson 2009: 42) 'What is the tallest tower you can build using only A4 paper and sticky tape? What happens if you use larger sheets?' engenders immediate enthusiasm and interest.

CREATIVE TEACHERS

Creative teachers remember the importance of fun. In the main this book has sought to emphasise 'hard fun' – helping children to find and solve problems, identify patterns, collaborate, discuss and think. But sometimes techniques and approaches which emphasise fun for its own sake can help children simply to remember some of the things that they find hard. The example below describes a group of children having fun, remembering square numbers.

Creative teachers acknowledge the nature of learning. Leighton *et al.* (2007: 132–3) uses the acronym RING to help students (and teachers) remember four key conditions for learning. Learning need to be *relevant* – if we don't understand the brain finds it hard to engage. It needs to be *interesting* – if you are not interested then you cannot recall. He suggests that learning also needs to be *naughty* and to make you *giggle* – the humour changes the chemistry of the brain and the images it evokes support visualisation – an aspect of abstract thinking. The example below describes some work in which RING was being explored.

> A Year 6 class was struggling to remember the difference between a parallelogram and a rhombus. The children were asked to imagine a little square in their hand. Then they were asked to think about it as a baby square wearing an all in one romper suit. They had time to think about what colour the romper suit was and also to imagine what was on the pocket of the romper suit. Then they held out their hands and admired their baby square in its bright red romper suit. Suddenly it fell over and the group called out the word rhombus. Next the class were asked to imagine a train speeding along parallel lines. They used their hands to demonstrate the train's movement, stretching out as far as they could go. Suddenly the train came off the track with a big crash. Moving the top hand forward over the bottom hand the class made a crashing noise and then called out parallelogram.

Creative teachers recognise the importance of space and time. Claxton (1997) emphasises the role of 'slow ways of knowing' in the creative process and this means creating opportunity, unhurried time and mental space to review children's learning with them (Mercer and Littleton 2007). Teachers also need to model this process – helping children to understand how to identify learning and how to review it (Lee 2006).

As we saw in Chapter 1 (Cremin 2010), creativity is not something we can develop in others unless we are prepared to nurture our own creativity. In order to be mathematically creative we have also to nurture our willingness to explore mathematical ideas. Teaching mathematics creatively will therefore require:

MEMORY TECHNIQUES

In *Success in the Creative Classroom* (Leighton *et al.* 2007: 136) Roy Leighton talks about how physical activities can engage the memory. He has created an exercise that involves visualising and placing imagined objects throughout the body. This technique can be used for anything that needs to be remembered.

Taking up this challenge MakeBelieve Arts tried the approach with a group of Year 6 children who were involved in revision of square numbers for the forthcoming SATs exam. The workshop leader and the Year 6 pupils worked together to create the following list of objects to remember the first 10 square numbers. The pupils then worked through the list, visualising each object and placing it on the relevant part of the body.

Square Number	Object	Explanation	Visualisation
1 × 1 = 1	Prize winning cup	Number 1 = winning	Place the winning cup on your HEAD
2 × 2 = 4	Door	Rhymes with four	Push a door into your EAR
3 × 3 = 9	A German man shaking head	German for no is NEIN	Hold a small German man shaking his head up to your EYE
4 × 4 = 16	Sweets	Sweet Sixteen	Push a favourite sweet up your NOSE
5 × 5 = 25	Christmas tree	25th is Christmas day	Put a miniature Christmas tree into your MOUTH
6 × 6 = 36	Twix	Rhymes with 36	Put a twix in your POCKET
7 × 7 = 49	A door with a German man shaking his head and knocking on it	Clever reincorporation by an 11-year-old boy Door = 4 German = Nein (see above)	Squash a door with a German man shaking his head between your KNEES
8 × 8 = 64	Old person	Song – when I'm 64	Balance an old person on your FEET
9 × 9 = 81	Arabic number on hand	If you look at your left hand it contains the Arabic number for 81*	Admire the Arabic number for 81 on your LEFT HAND
10 × 10 = 100	The Queen	When you get to 100 years of age you get a birthday card from the Queen	Hold the Queen in your RIGHT HAND

* Note: You can check out how to visualise the Arabic symbol for 81 on your left hand by going to http://img221.imageshack.us/img221/7223/palmh1qe2.jpg.

The group spent time going visualising these numbers, then we repeated it later on in the session. MakeBelieve Arts was back with the group a week later and to their amazement the children had good recall of square numbers.

- belief in play and narrative as the bedrock of all human understanding and abstract thought;
- maintenance of the childlike curiosity that maintains a sense of wonder at the world about us, actively seeking and solving problems;
- collaboration with parents, colleagues and children;
- an enjoyment of challenge and 'hard fun' together with a spirit of flexibility and a measure of spontaneity to ensure that learning opportunities are not lost.

FURTHER READING

Duckworth, E. (ed.) (2001) *Tell Me More*. New York: Teachers' College Press.
Lee, C. (2006) *Language for Learning Mathematics*. Maidenhead: Open University Press.
Wyse, D. and Dowson, P. (2009) *The Really Useful Creativity Book*. London: Routledge.

CHILDREN'S BOOKS

McNaughton, C. and Kitamura, S. (2005) *Once Upon an Ordinary School Day*, London: Andersen Press Ltd.
This book is not about mathematics but it is about creative teaching. Through his creative teaching, the supply teacher changes the dull greyness of a child's life to an extraordinary world of excitement and colour.

BIBLIOGRAPHY

Alexander, R. (ed.) (2010) *Children, their World, their Education*. London: Routledge.

Allan, T. (2009) *Myths of the World*. London: Duncan Baird Publishers.

Alperin, R. (2000) 'A mathematical theory of origami constructions and numbers', *New York Journal of Mathematics,* 6: 119–33.

Andrews, A. and Trafton, P. (2002) *Little Kids – Powerful Problem Solvers*. Portsmouth, NH: Heinemann.

Anghileri, J. (2001) *Principles and Practices in Arithmetic Teaching*. Buckingham: Open University Press.

Anning, A. and Ring, K. (2004) *Making Sense of Children's Drawing*. Maidenhead: Open University Press.

Atkinson, S. (1992) *Mathematics with Reason*. London: Hodder and Stoughton.

Bearne, E. and Wolstencraft, H. (2007) *Visual Approaches to Teaching Writing: Multimodal Literacy 5–11*. London: Paul Chapman Publishing/United Kingdom Literacy Association.

Becta (2009) Becta's contribution to the *Rose Review*, available at http://publication.becta.org.uk (accessed 7 May 2010). Becta: Coventry.

Berlinghoff, W. and Gouvea, F. (2004) *Math Through the Ages*. Farmington ME: Oxton House Publishers.

Blakeslee, S. and Blakeslee, M. (2007) *The Body Has a Mind of Its Own*. New York: Random House.

Boaler, J. (2009) *The Elephant in the Classroom*. London: Souvenir Press Ltd.

Booth, J. and Siegler, R. (2008) 'Numerical magnitude representations influence arithmetical learning', *Child Development*, 79: 1016–31.

Bower, T. (1977) *The Perceptual World of the Child*. London: Fontana.

Bowkett, S., Lee, T., Harding, T. and Leighton, R. (2007) *Success in the Creative Classroom*. London: Network Continuum Education.

Brandon, K., Hall, N. and Taylor, D. (1993) *Math Through Children's Literature*. Santa Barbara CA: Libraries Unlimited Inc.

Brandt, P. A. (2009) 'Music and how we became human: a view from cognitive semiotics', in S. Malloch and C. Trevarthen (eds) *Communicative Musicality*. Oxford: Oxford University Press.

Bresler, L. (2004) *Knowing Bodies: Moving Minds*. Dordrecht, The Netherlands: Kluwer Academic Publishers.

Bruner, J. (1986) *Actual Minds, Possible Worlds*. London: Harvard University Press.

Butterworth, B. (1999) *The Mathematical Brain*. London: MacMillan.

Butterworth, B. (2005) 'The development of arithmetical abilities', *Journal of Child Psychology and Psychiatry*, 46: 1003–18.

Cairns, W. (2007) *About the Size of It*. London: Macmillan.

Carson, J., Burks, V., Parke, R. and MacDonald, K. (1993) *Parent-Child Physical Play: Determinants and Consequences*. Albany: State University of New York Press.

Castagnetti, M. and Vecchi, V. (1997) *Shoe and Meter*. Reggio Emilia: Reggio Children.

Claxton, G. (1997) *Hare Brain: Tortoise Mind*. London: Fourth Estate.

Claxton, G. (2000) 'The anatomy of intuition', in T. Atkinson and G. Claxton (eds) *The Intuitive Practitioner*. Buckingham: Open University Press.

Claxton, G. (2008) *What's the Point of School?* Oxford: One World Publications.

Clements, D. (2000) 'Concrete manipulatives: concrete ideas', *Contemporary Issues in Early Childhood*, 1(1): 45–60.

Clements, D. (2004) 'Major themes and recommendations', in D. Clements and J. Sarama (eds) *Engaging Young Children in Mathematics*. London: Lawrence Erlbaum Associates.

Cobb, E. (1977) *The Ecology of Imagination in Childhood*. Putnam CT: Columbia University Press.

Craft, A. (2005) *Creativity in Schools: Tensions and Dilemmas*. London: Routledge.

Craft, A., Cremin, T., Burnard, P. and Chappell, K. (2007) 'Teacher stories in creative learning: a study of progression', *Thinking Skills and Creativity*, 2(2): 136–47.

Cremin, T. (2010) *Teaching English Creatively*. London: Routledge.

Croydon Beam Group (2004) *Starting from Big Numbers*. London: BEAM Publications.

Csikszentmihalyi, M. (1997) *Creativity*. London: HarperPerennial.

Daniel, M. F. (1999) 'A primary school curriculum to foster thinking about mathematics', *Canadian Journal of Education*, 24(4): 426–40.

de Bono, E. (1995) *Serious Creativity: Using the Power of Lateral Thinking to Create New Ideas*. London: HarperCollins Publishers Ltd.

Dehaene, S. (1997) *The Number Sense: How the Mind Creates Mathematics*. London: Allen Press.

Demaine, E. and O'Rourke, J. (2008) *Geometric Folding Algorithms*. Cambridge: Cambridge University Press.

Department for Children, Schools and Families (DCSF) (2008) *Mark-making Matters*. Nottingham: DCSF Publications.

DES (Department for Education and Science) (1982) *Mathematics Counts* (Cockcroft Report). London: HMSO.

Devi, S. (1977) *Figuring*. London: Penguin Group.

Devlin, K. (2000) *The Maths Gene*. London: Weidenfeld and Nicolson.

Devlin, K. (2002) *The Language of Mathematics*. New York: Holt Paperback.

DfEE (Department for Education and Employment) (1999a) *The National Curriculum: Handbook for Primary Teachers in England*. London: HMSO.

DfEE (1999b) *The National Numeracy Strategy*. Sudbury: DfEE Publications.

DfES (Department for Education and Skills) (2003) *Excellence and Enjoyment – A Strategy for Primary Schools*. Nottingham: DfES Publications.

DfES (2006a) *Learning Outside the Classroom Manifesto*. Available at http://www.lotc.org.uk/getmedia/42c7c3e7–7455–43cc-a513-d6aef9654846/1.0-Learning-Outside-the-Classroom-manifesto.aspx (accessed 10 February 2010). Nottingham: DfES Publications.

DfES (2006b) *Primary National Strategy: Primary Framework for Literacy and Mathematics*. Nottingham: DfES Publications.

DfES (2007) *Early Years Foundation Stage Guidance*. Sudbury: DfES Publications.

Donaldson, M. (1976) *Children's Minds*. London: Fontana.

Drummond, M-J. (2003) *Assessing Children's Learning*. London: David Fulton.

Duckworth, E. (1996) *'The Having of Wonderful Ideas' and Other Essays on Teaching and Learning*. New York: Teachers' College Press.

Duckworth, E. (ed.) (2001*)* *Tell Me More*. New York: Teachers' College Press.

du Sautoy, M. (2004) *The Music of the Primes*. London: HarperPerennial.
du Sautoy, M. (2008a) 'I'm not very fast at my times tables', available at http://www.guardian.co.uk/science/2008/nov/03/marcus-dusautoy (accessed 7 May 2010).
du Sautoy, M. (2008b) *Symmetry: A Journey into the Patterns of Nature*. New York: HarperCollins Perennial.
du Sautoy, M. (2009) 'The trillion dollar question', available at http://www.guardian.co.uk/world/2009/mar/25/trillion-dollar-rescue-plan (accessed 7 May 2010).
du Sautoy, M. (2010) 'Maths maketh the man', *Education Guardian*, 19 January.
Edwards, C., Gandini, L. and Forman, G. (1998) *The Hundred Languages of Children: the Reggio Emilia Approach to Early Childhood Education* (2nd edn). Norwood, NJ: Ablex Publishing Corporation.
Egan, K. (1988) *Teaching as Storytelling*. London: Routledge.
Egan, K. (1991) *Primary Understanding*. London: Routledge.
Eliot, L. (1999) *Early Intelligence*. London: Penguin.
Fisher, R. (2005) *Teaching children to Think* (2nd edn). London: Nelson Thornes.
Flannery, S. (2002) *In Code: A Mathematical Journey*. Chapel Hill: Algonquin Books.
Froebel Block Play Research Group (1992) 'Being mathematical', In P. Gura (ed.) *Exploring Learning*. London: Paul Chapman Publishing.
Fuson, K. (2004) 'Pre-K to grade 2 goals and standards: achieving 21st century mastery for all', in D. Clements and J. Sarama (eds) *Engaging Young Children in Mathematics*. Mahwah, NJ: Lawrence Erlbaum Associates Inc.
Gardner, H. (1999) *Intelligence Reframed*. New York: Basic Books.
Gardner, H. (2006) *Five Minds for the Future*. Boston, MA: Harvard Business School Press.
Gerhardt, S. (2004) *Why Love Matters*. Hove: Brunner Routledge.
Gifford, S. (2005) *Teaching Mathematics 3–5*. Maidenhead: Open University Press.
Goldschmied, E. and Selleck, D. (1996) *Communication Between Babies in Their First Year* (video). London: National Children's Bureau.
Goleman, D. (1996) *Emotional Intelligence*. London: Fontana.
Gopnik, A., Melfzoff, A. and Kuhl, P. (1999) *How Babies Think*. London: Weidenfeld and Nicolson.
Greenfield, S. (2004) *Tomorrow's People*. London: Penguin Press.
Gura, P. (ed.) (1992) *Exploring Learning*. London: Paul Chapman Publishing.
Hallam, S. (2001) *The Power of Music*. London: Performing Rights Society.
Hardy, G. H. (1992) *The Mathematician's Apology*. Cambridge: Cambridge University Press (first published 1941).
Hargreaves, D. (2004) Keynote lecture *National Association of Music Educators Conference*, London 17–19 September.
Harriman, H. (2008) *The Outdoor Classroom*. Swindon: Corner to Learn.
Harkleroad, L. (2006) *The Math Behind the Music*. New York: Cambridge University Press.
Haven, K. (2007) *Story Proof: the Science behind the Startling Power of Story*. Westport, CT: Libraries Unlimited.
Haven, K. (nd) *Voice of the Mind*, available at http://esdepo.gsfc.nasa.gov/docs/files/20060503_Haven_Kendall.pdf (accessed 7 May 2010).
Healy, J. (1999) *Failure to Connect*. New York: Touchstone.
Heathcote, D. and Bolton, G. (1996) *Drama for Learning, Dorothy Heathcote's Mantle of the Expert Approach to Education*. Westport: Greenwood Press.
Heuvel-Panhuizen,M. (2008) 'Learning from "didactikids": an impetus for revisiting the empty number line', *Mathematics Education Research Journal*, 20(3): 6–31.
Hilliam R. (2004) *Galileo: Father of Modern Science, Opere Il Saggiatore*. New York: Rosen Publishing Group.
Howe, M. (1999) *Genius Explained*. Cambridge; Cambridge University Press.
Hughes, M. (1986) *Children and Number*. Oxford: Basil Blackwell.
Isaacson, W. (2007) *Einstein: His Life and Universe*. London: Simon and Schuster.

Kanade, T. (1980) 'A theory of origami world', *Artificial Intelligence*, 13(3): 279–311.

Keenan, T. (2002) *An Introduction to Child Development*. London: Sage.

Knight, S. (2009) *Forest Schools and Outdoor Learning in the Early Years*. London: Sage.

Kress, G. (1996) *Before Writing*. London: Routledge.

Kress, G. (2003) *Literacy in the New Media Age*. Trowbridge: Cromwell Press.

LeDoux, J. (1998) *The Emotional Brain*. London: Weidenfeld and Nicolson.

Lee, C. (2006) *Language for Learning Mathematics*. Maidenhead: Open University Press.

Lee, T, (2003) *A Little or a Lot,* Book 1, Dramatic Mathematics Series, MakeBelieve Arts publication, available at http://www.makebelievearts.co.uk (accessed 7 May 2010).

Leighton, R., Lee, T., Harding, T. and Bowkett, S. (2007) *Success in the Creative Classroom*. London: Network Continuum Education.

Lipman, M. (2003) *Thinking in Education*. Cambridge: Cambridge University Press.

Lonegreen, S. (2001) *Labyrinths*. New York: Sterling Publishing Co. Inc.

Louv, R. (2006) *Last Child in the Woods*. New York: Algonquin Books.

Lucas, B. (2001) *Power up your Mind*. London: Nicholas Brealey Publishing.

MacGregor, H. (1998) *Tom Thumb's Musical Maths*. London: A&C Black.

MacGregor, H. and Gargreave, B. (2001) *Let's Go Zudie-o*. London: A&C Black.

MacGregor, H. and Gargreave, B. (2004) *Let's Go Shoolie-Shoo*. London: A&C Black.

Malaguzzi, L. (1995) 'History, ideas and basic philosophy', in C. Edwards, L. Gandini and G. Forman (eds) *The Hundred Languages of Children.* Norwood, NJ: Ablex Publishing Corporation.

Malloch, S. and Trevarthen, C. (2009) *Communicative Musicality*. Oxford: Oxford University Press.

Marsh, J., Brooks, G., Hughes, J., Ritichie, L., Roberts, S. and Wright, K. (2005) *Digital Beginnings Report*. BBC Worldwide/Esmee Fairbairn Foundation, available at http://www.esmeefairbairn.org.uk/docs/DigitalBeginningsReport.pdf (accessed 7 May 2010).

Marsh, J. and Hallet, E. (2008) *Desirable Literacies* (2nd edn). London: Sage.

Matthews, G. (1980) *Philosophy and the Young Child*. Cambridge, MA: Harvard University Press.

Matthews, J. (2003) *Drawing and Painting*. London: Paul Chapman Publishing.

Mazur, B. (2003) *Imagining Numbers*. London: Allen Lane.

Meek, M. (1992) *On Being Literate*. Portsmouth, NH: Heinemann.

Mercer, N. and Littleton, K. (2007) *Dialogue and the Development of Children's Thinking*. Abingdon, Oxon: Routledge.

Mithen, S. (2005) *The Singing Neanderthals*. London: Weidenfeld and Nicholson.

Moyer, P. (2001) 'Are we having fun yet? How to use manipulatives to teach mathematics', *Education Studies in Mathematics*, 47(2): 175–97.

Moyer, P., Bolyard, J. and Spikell, M. (2002) 'What are virtual manipulatives?' *Teaching Children Mathematics*, 8(6): 372–7.

Moyles, J. (1989) *Just Playing*. Milton Keynes: Open University Press.

NACCCE (1999) *All Our Futures, Creativity, Culture and Education*. Sudbury: DfEE Publications.

Namy, L. L. (ed.) (2005) *Symbol Use and Symbolic Representation*. Mahwah, NJ: Lawrence Erlbaum Associates Inc.

National Council of Teachers of Mathematics (NCTM) (2000) *Principles and Standards for School Mathematics*. Reston, VA: NCTM.

National Strategies (2006) *Reviewing the Primary Framework for Mathematics: Discussion Paper*, available at http://nationalstrategies.standards.dcsf.gov.uk/node/47104 (accessed 7 May 2010).

National Strategies (2009a) 'So what is mathematics? Guidance paper: mathematics and the primary curriculum', available at http://nationalstrategies.standards.dcsf.gov.uk/print/18690 (accessed 7 May 2010).

National Strategies (2009b) *Numbers and patterns: Laying Foundations in Mathematics*. London: DCSF.

Newton, E. (2009) *The Power of Origami*, available at http://plus.maths.org/issue53/features/newton/index.html (accessed 7 May 2010).

Nixon, H. and Comber, B. (2005) 'Behind the scenes: making movies in early years classrooms', in J. Marsh (ed.) *Popular Culture, Media and Digital Literacies in Early Childhood*. London: Routledge.

Nunes, T., Carraher, D. and Schliemann, A. D. (1993) *Street Mathematics and School Mathematics*. Cambridge: Cambridge University Press.

O'Malley, C. (2007) *Leonardo da Vinci on the Human Body*. London: Crown Publications.

Odam, G. (1995) *The Sounding Symbol*. Cheltenham: Stanley Thornes.

Ofsted (2005) 'National Strategies are having a positive impact in primary and secondary schools' (reference no: NR-2005–87), available at http://www.ofsted.gov.uk (accessed 10 February 2010).

Ofsted (2010) *Learning: Creative Approaches That Raise Standards*, available at http://www.ofsted.gov.uk/publications/080266 (accessed 7 June 2010).

Organisation for Economic Co-operation and Development (OECD) (1999) *Measuring Student Knowledge and Skills: A New Framework for Assessment*. Paris: OECD Publication Service.

Paley, V. G. (1981) *Wally's Stories*. London: Harvard University Press.

Paley, V. G. (1990) *The Boy Who Would Be A Helicopter*. Cambridge MA: Harvard University Press.

Paley, V. G. (1997) *Story and Play The Original Learning Tools,* lecture given 10 March, Walferdange, Luxembourg, available at http://www.script.lu/documentation/archiv/decoprim/paley.htm (accessed 7 May 2010).

Paley, V. G. (2004) *A Child's Work: The Importance of Fantasy Play*. London: The University of Chicago Press.

Pallasmaa, J. (2005) *The Eyes of the Skin*. Chichester: John Wiley and Sons.

Papert, S. (1982) *Mindstorms*. Brighton: Harvester Press.

Pinker, S. (2000) *Words and Rules*. London: Orion Books Ltd.

Pound, L. (2005) *How Children Learn*. Leamington Spa: Step Forward Publishing.

Pound, L. (2006) *Supporting Mathematical Development in the Early Years* (2nd edn). Maidenhead: Open University Press.

Pound, L. (2008) *Thinking and Learning about Mathematics in the Early Years*. London: Nursery World/Routledge.

Pound, L. (2009) *How Children Learn 3*. London: Practical Pre-school.

Pound, L. and Harrison, C. (2003) *Supporting Musical Development in the Early Years*. Maidenhead: Open University Press.

Pringle, E. (2008) 'Artists' perspectives on art practice and pedagogy', in J. Sefton-Green (ed.) *Creative Learning*. London: Arts Council England.

Qualifications and Curriculum Authority (QCA) (2004) *Creativity Find It! Promote It! – Promoting Pupils' Creative Thinking and Behaviour Across the Curriculum at Key Stages 1, 2 and 3 – Practical Materials for Schools*. London: QCA.

Ramachandran,V. S. (2004) *A Brief Tour of Consciousness*. New York: Pearson Education Inc.

Ramachandran, V. S. and Blakeslee, S. (1999) *Phantoms in the Brain*. London: Fourth Estate Ltd.

Read, J. (1992) 'A short history of children's building blocks', in P. Gura (ed.) *Exploring Learning*. London: Paul Chapman Publishing

Resnick, L. B. (1988) 'Treating mathematics as an ill-structured discipline', in R. I. Charles and E. A. Silver (eds) *The Teaching and Assessing of Mathematical Problem Solving*. Hillsdale, NJ: Lawrence Erlbaum Associates, pp. 32–60.

Resnik, M. (1999) *Mathematics as a Science of Patterns*. Oxford: Oxford University Press.

Rhydderch-Evans, Z. (1993) *Mathematics in the School Grounds*. Winchester: Learning through Landscapes/Crediton: Southgate Publishers Ltd.

Rizzolatti, G. and Craighero, L. (2005) 'Mirror neurons: a neurological approach to empathy', *Neurobiology of Human Values*: 107–23.

Robinson, K. (2001) *Out of Our Minds: Learning to Be Creative*. Oxford: Capstone Press.

Rogoff, B. (2003) *The Cultural Nature of Human Development*. Oxford: Oxford University Press.

Ronan, M. (2007) *Symmetry and the Monster*. Oxford: Oxford University Press.

Rose, J. (2009) *Independent Review of the Primary Curriculum: Final Report*. London: DCSF.

Schiro, M. (2004) *Oral Storytelling and Teaching Mathematics*. London: Sage Publications Ltd.

Siegel, D. (1999) *The Developing Mind*. New York: Guilford Press.

Singh, S. (1997) *Fermat's Last Theorem*. London: Fourth Estate.

Skinner, C. (2005) *Maths Outdoors*. London: BEAM Publications.

Smith, C. (2005) 'The CD-ROM game: a toddler engaged in computer-based dramatic play', in J. March (ed.) *Popular Culture, New Media and Digital Literacy in Early Childhood*. London: Routledge.

Smolucka, L. and Smolucka, F. (1998) 'The social origins of mind: post-Piagetian perspectives on pretend play', in O. Saracho and B. Spodek (eds) *Multiple Perspectives on Play in Early Childhood Education*. Albany: State University of New York.

Stevens, J. (2008) *Maths in Stories*. London: BEAM Education Ltd.

Sylva, K., Bruner, J. and Genova, P. (1976) 'The role of play in the problem-solving of children 3–5 years old', in J. Bruner, A. Jolly and K. Sylva (eds) *Play: Its Role in Development and Evolution*. Harmondsworth, Middlesex: Penguin Books.

Tizard, B. and Hughes, M. (1986) *Young Children Learning*. London: Fontana.

Tovey, H. (2007) *Playing Outdoors*. Maidenhead: Open University Press.

Tower Hamlets (2009) *More to Maths than Counting*. London: LB of Tower Hamlets.

Trickey, S. (2007) 'Promoting thinking for learning through collaborative enquiry: an evaluation of 'thinking through philosophy', available at http://www.sapere.org.uk (accessed 10 February 2010).

Upitis, R., Phillips, E. and Higginson, W. (1997) *Creative Mathematics*. London: Routledge.

Uttal, D., Scudder, K. and DeLoache, J. (1997) 'Manipulatives as symbols', *Journal of Applied Developmental Psychology*, 18(1): 37–54.

Vorderman, C. (2010) 'Notable number crunchers', *Education Guardian*, 19 January.

Vygotsky, L. (1978) *The Mind in Society*. Cambridge, MA: Harvard University Press.

Vygotsky, L. (1986) *Thought and Language*. London: MIT Press.

Walsh, J. and Sattes, E. (2005) *Quality Questioning: Research-based Practice to Engage Every Learner*. Thousand Oaks CA: Corwin Press.

Wardle, F. (2002) *Introduction to Early Childhood Education*. Boston, MA: Allyn and Bacon.

White, J. (2008) *Playing and Learning Outdoors*. London: Routledge/Nursery World.

Whitehead, M. (2009) *Supporting the Development of Language and Literacy in the Early Years* (2nd edn). Maidenhead: Open University Press.

Whitin, D. and Wilde, S. (1995) *It's The Story That Counts*. Portsmouth, NH: Heinemann.

Williams, H. (2006) *Let's Pretend Maths*. London: BEAM Publications.

Wood, D. (1988) *How Children Think and Learn*. Oxford: Blackwell.

Worthington, M. and Carruthers, E. (2006) *Children's Mathematics: Making Marks, Making Meaning*. London: Sage.

Wyse, D. and Dowson, P. (2009) *The Really Useful Creative Book*. Abingdon, Oxon: Routledge.

Zuckerman, O., Arida, S. and Resnick, M. (2005) 'Extending tangible interfaces for education: digital Montessori-inspired manipulatives', *Proceedings of the SIGCHI Conference on Human Factors in Computing Systems*. New York: Association for Computing Machinery.

CHILDREN'S BOOKS

Agard, J. (2003) *Einstein: The Girl Who Hated Maths*. London: Hodder Children's Books.
Allen, P. (1988) *Who Sank the Boat?* London: Puffin Books.
Allen, P. (1994) *Mr Archimedes' Bath*. London: Picture Puffins.
Anno, M. (1999) *Anno's Magic Seeds*. New York: Penguin Putnam Books for Young Readers.
Anno, M. and Anno, M. (1999) *Anno's Mysterious Multiplying Jar*. New York: Penguin Putnam Books for Young Readers.
Briggs, R. (1973) *Jim and the Beanstalk*. London: Picture Puffins.
Brown, P. (1993) *Moon Jump a Cowntdown*. London: Penguin Books Ltd.
Butterworth, N. (2003a) *The Secret Path*. London: Collins Picture Books.
Butterworth, N. (2003b) *The Treasure Hunt*. London: Collins Picture Books.
Clement, R. (1995) *Counting on Frank*. Boston: Houghton Mifflin.
Clements, G. (2007) *A Picture History of Great Buildings*. London: Frances Lincoln Children's Books.
Crowther, R. (2002) *Shapes*. London: Walker Books
Dahl, R. and Blake, Q. (2001) *The BFG*. Harmondsworth: Puffin Fiction.
Daniel, M.-F., Lafortune, L., Pallascio, R. and Sykes, P. (1996) *Les Aventures mathématiques de Mathilde et David*. Quebec: Le Loup de Gouttière.
Dee, R. (1990) *Two Ways to Count to Ten*. New York: Henry Holt and Co.
Donaldson, J. and Pichon, L. (2002) *Spinderella*. London: Egmont UK Ltd.
Donaldson, J. and Scheffler, A. (2002) *The Smartest Giant in Town* London: Macmillan.
Dunbar, J. and Dunbar, P. (2005) *Shoe Baby*. London: Walker Books.
Enzensberger, H. (2008) *The Number Devil*. London: Granta Publications.
Farley, J. (1997) *Giant Hiccups*. London: Tamarind Books.
Fox, D. (1998*) People At Work: Making a Film*. London: Evans Bros Ltd.
Fromental, J-L. and Jolivet, J. (2006) *365 Penguins*. New York: Abrams Books for Young Children.
Gravett, E. (2009) *The Rabbit Problem*. London: Macmillan Children's Books.
Gray, K. and Sharratt, N. (2001) *Eat Your Peas*. London: Red Fox Books.
Herrmann, F. and Him, G. (1986) *All about the Giant Alexander*. London: Piccolo.
Horacek, P. (2004) *A New House for Mouse*. London: Walker Books.
Hughes, T. (1994) *The Iron Woman*. London: Faber Children's Books.
Hughes, T. (2005) *The Iron Man*. London: Faber Children's Books.
Hutchins, P. (1987) *Changes, Changes*. New York: Aladdin Paperbacks.
Hutchins, P. (1989) *The Doorbell Rang*. London: Harper Trophy.
Inkpen, M. (1998) *The Great Pet Sale*. London: Hodder Children's Books.
Jenkins, S. (2006) *Actual Size*. London: Frances Lincoln Children's Books.
Johmann, C. and Rieth, E. (1999) *Bridges: Amazing Structures to Design, Build and Test*. Charlotte Vermont: Williamson Publishing Company.
Johmann, C. and Rieth, E. (2001) *Skyscrapers: Amazing Structures to Design, Build and Test*. Charlotte Vermont: Williamson Publishing Company.
Jones, R. (2009) *See Inside Famous Buildings*. London: Usborne.
McNaughton, C. and Kitamura, S. (2005) *Once Upon An Ordinary School Day*. London: Andersen Press Ltd.
Milbourne A. and Riglietti, S. (2007) *How Big is a Million?* London: Usborne Publishing Ltd.
Moore, I. (2000) *Six Dinner Sid*. London: Hodder Children's Books.
Pappas, T. (1997) *The Adventures of Penrose the Mathematical Cat*. San Carlos, CA: Wide World Publishing.
Pinczes, J. (1993) *One Hundred Hungry Ants*. New York: Houghton Mifflin Co.
Pouyet, M. (2006) *Artistes de Nature*. Toulouse: Editions Plume de Carotte.
Rempt, F. and Smit, N. (2006) *Snail's Birthday Wish*. London: Boxer Books.
Reynolds, P. (2007*) So Few of Me*. London: Walker Books.

Roeder, A. (2009) *13 Buildings Children Should Know*. London: Prestel.
Ross, T. (2002) *Centipede's 100 Shoes*. London: Andersen Press Ltd.
Ross, T. (2008) *I'm Coming To Get You*. London: Picture Puffins.
Sayre, A. and Sayre, J. (2006) *One is a Snail Ten is a Crab*. Somerville, MA: Candlewick Press.
Scamell, R. and Terry, M. (2006) *Ouch!* London: Little Tiger Press.
Scieszka, J. and Smith, L. (1995) *Math Curse*. London: Penguin Books.
Schwartz, D. (1985) *How Much is a Million?* New York: Harper Trophy.
Steer, D. (1996) *Mythical Mazes*. Andover, Hants: Templar Books.
Swift, J. (1993) *Gulliver's Travels*. Bath: Parragon Book Service.
Swift, J. (1994) *Gulliver's Travels* London: Penguin Popular Classics.
Thorne-Thomsen, K. (1994) *Frank Lloyd Wright for Kids*. Chicago: Chicago Review Press.
Vernon Lloyd, J. (1988) *The Giant Jam Sandwich*. London: Piper Picture Books.
Walker, R. and Sharkey, N. (1999) *Jack and the Beanstalk*. Bath: Barefoot Books.
Wenzel, A. (2010) *13 Sculptures Children Should Know*. London: Prestel.
Wilde, O. (1982) *The Selfish Giant*. Harmondsworth: Picture Puffin.
Williams, B. and Fatus, S. (2008) *The Real Princess*. Bath: Barefoot Books.

INDEX